YOUR BOOK IN BOOKSTORES

ALLI'S GUIDE TO PRINT BOOK DISTRIBUTION FOR AUTHORS

DEBBIE P. YOUNG
ALLIANCE OF INDEPENDENT AUTHORS

CONTENTS

A Note About ALLi   v

1. About This Book   1
2. Terms of Reference   7
3. How Bookstores Operate   13
4. Why Bother with Bookstores?   19
5. Physical Bookstores Today   27
6. Different Types of Bookstore   41
7. How Bookstores Operate   55
8. Make Your Book Bookstore Ready   71
9. How to Pitch Your Book   91
10. Bookstore Book Launches   99
11. Financial Considerations   107
12. Other Ways of Selling Print Books   119
13. How I Do It   127
14. Bookstores in the Community   141
15. Going Forward Together   147

THE END

Appendix I: Bookstores in Books   151

APPENDIX II: GLOSSARY OF SELF-PUBLISHING TERMS

#	155
A	157
B	167
C	177
D	187
E	193
F	199
G	203
H	207
I	211
J	217
K	219
L	223

M	227
N	231
O	235
P	237
Q	247
R	249
S	253
T	265
U	269
V	273
W	275
X	279
Y	281
Z	283
Index	285

THE END

Acknowledgments	299
Join ALLi	301

MORE ADVICE & FEEDBACK

Advice Updates from ALLi	305
Creative Business Planning Membership & Workshops	307
We'd love your feedback	309

A NOTE ABOUT ALLI
THE ALLIANCE OF INDEPENDENT AUTHORS

This book is one of a number of self-publishing guidebooks and campaign books for authors produced by the Alliance of Independent Authors (ALLi).

If you haven't yet heard of ALLi, it is a global, non-profit association for self-publishing authors. Our mission is ethics and excellence in self-publishing and we bring together thousands of indie authors all over the world who are united behind this mission.

All our profits are reinvested back into the organization for the benefit of our members—and the wider author community.

ALLi is pronounced "ally" (al-eye), and an ally is what we aim to be to self-publishers everywhere. Our name is spelt with a big ALL and small i because our members are like the three musketeers in Dumas's eponymous novel: ALL working for each individual "i", and each for ALL.

ALLi offers members a range of benefits but our real strength is our members, team and advisors, who provide something like the ancient system of craft apprenticeship, with the wisdom of the hive-mind instead of one master.

Our work is fourfold:

A Note About ALLi

- ALLi *advises*, providing best-practice information and education through a Self-Publishing Advice Center that offers a daily blog, weekly livestreams and podcasts, a bookstore of self-publishing guidebooks, and a quarterly member magazine.
- ALLi *monitors* the self-publishing sector through a **watchdog desk**, alerting authors to bad actors and predatory players and running an approved partner program.
- ALLi *campaigns* for the **advancement of indie authors** in the publishing and literary sectors globally (bookstores, libraries, literary events, prizes, grants, awards, and other author organizations), encouraging the provision of publishing and business skills for authors, speaking out against iniquities, and furthering the indie author cause wherever possible.
- ALLi *empowers* independent authors through a wide variety of **member tools and resources** including author forums, contract advice, sample agreements, networking, literary agency representation, and a member care desk.

Headquartered in London, we operate all over the world and at every level, bringing our mission of ethics and excellence in self-publishing to beginner, emerging and experienced authors. Whether you're just starting out, or you're already widely published, ALLi can empower you to make better books, reach more readers, and generate greater profits.

When you join ALLi, you're not just joining an organization, you're becoming part a transformative, self-organising, global author movement. Whether you're self-publishing your first novel or your fiftieth, ALLi is with you every step of the way, with a suite of member benefits that includes free guidebooks, discounts and deals, member forums, contract consultancy, advisory board, literary agency, watchdog and more.

Your membership also supports our advocacy work for indie authors globally, from Alaska to New Zealand and offers access to ALLi's supportive, dynamic community.

A Note About ALLi

If you haven't yet, is it time you joined us?
AllianceIndependentAuthors.org

1

ABOUT THIS BOOK

Once upon a time, bookstores were just about the only place that books were sold, in a choice of two formats: paperback or hardback. Then along came four revolutions:

- **Online shopping:** The arrival of the internet made online shopping from home not only possible but also popular, with books a particularly suitable commodity for this route, being easy to pack and mail, unbreakable in transit, and of consistent quality wherever you buy them.

- **Print-on-demand (POD) services:** Advances in digital printing technology made it possible for the first time to print good-quality books at a viable unit cost for resale at a profit in very short print runs.

- **Online publishing services:** The launch of various services enabled aspiring self-publishing authors to write, edit, design, format, and upload books without leaving their desk. (ALLi recommends outsourcing any tasks in which you can't achieve a professional standard yourself to provide a top-quality end product.)

- **The ereader:** First emerging in the form of a dedicated ereader, quickly joined by ereading apps for your preferred digital device, the ereader created a whole new market, offering indie authors a new low-cost, high-profit route to get their work in front of readers around the world at the touch of a button.

- **Digital Audio Technology:** Sound recordings no longer need to be turned into vinyl, tape or CD, but can be recorded, stored, manipulated, generated and reproduced using audio signals encoded in digital form.

These developments were enough to shake up the old worlds of publishing and bookselling on a seismic scale, providing booksellers with a whole new world of competition as well as a new diversity of products, all unendorsed by their usual suppliers, traditional publishing houses.

The problem is not that booksellers are Luddites—their business is powered by sophisticated just-in-time stock control and ordering systems—but many were concerned that the brave new ebook world would erode their core business. Indeed, a few bookstores gamely tried to make inroads into selling ebooks and ereaders, but with little success, and for the most part quietly withdrew from that sphere.

Then more recently, two further developments came along, making the marketplace even more complex but also more exciting:

- digital audio technolog
- subscription reading services for both audio and ebook.

Both of these innovations are changing readers habits, both in terms of how they read and how they buy.

The New Wave of Audiobooks

Audiobooks on tape and CD are legacy products. Audio is now accessed through digital download and easy to access via various smart devices. The rise of synchronised reading/listening experiences across both audio and ebook platform (read a chapter on your tablet in bed, listen to the next in your car as you drive to the station, then hear the next on your phone on your train ride to work), is seeing audio capturing a greater share of the book market than ever before.

Subscription models with a cut-price audiobook every month, and special deals for buying the matching ebook, make it a seductive offer.

The Rise of Subscription Reading

Subscription reading for ebooks encourages an "all you can eat for on low price" mentality, with readers signing up to borrow, library-style, a set number of books for a low monthly financial commitment, as an alternative to buying ebooks, print or audio outright. Amazon's Kindle Unlimited is the most well-known and widespread of these, other online retailers offer competitive services such as Kobo Plus.

The Rise and Fall of In-store Book Printing

While these last two changes were bubbling under, some commentators identified a further new development that might offer bookstores an easy inroad to this brave new digital world: the Espresso Book Machine owned by OnDemandBooks.com, as a means by which booksellers could embrace the digital arena. These sophisticated digital printers produce POD books on the spot, drawing content from remote databases, in the time that it takes to brew a cup of coffee.

Enthusiasts (and sales staff) suggested the technology would also empower booksellers to produce books whose content was in the public domain, such as out-of-copyright classics, at a substantial markup. A further market would be high-value, low-volume publications such as academic theses.

In theory, this sounded promising. The Espresso would allow the bookstore to become a direct producer and distributor, while offering the reader instant access to digitally printed books within their local physical bookstore, cutting out the internet intermediary.

Unfortunately, the enormous cost of these highly sophisticated machines is way beyond the budget of the average bookstore. Return on investment is long and slow, even in highly populous cities, never mind issues of maintenance and repair, compared with the relatively simple photocopier. They also have a limited range that all POD systems have – small choice of interior and cover stock, narrow range of sizes, etc. No surprises, then, that this has not proved to be a fairy godmother for bookstores, enabling them to leap aboard the digital revolution.

As these recent developments bed down with publishers, booksellers and authors alike, the options for indie authors have broadened. A few years ago, many self-publishing authors, particularly early adopters of the digital technologies, decided to bypass print books altogether, given the higher potential profit margins on ebooks, whose production costs were entirely front-loaded, and whose delivery and inventory costs were nil.

As it gradually became clear that the rise of the ebook did not spell the decline and ultimate extinction of print, most authors realised that if they didn't also offer a print option, they'd be missing out on a significant chunk of potential business.

Now a growing number feel compelled also to embrace audio – despite the very high outlay required to produce audiobooks (Findaway Voices currently estimates $250 per recorded hour as a rough guide) so as not to miss out on the diversification of the reading market.

Those indie authors who did embrace print, via POD services, often found it nigh on impossible to get their books into bookstores, which were entirely geared up to dealing only with big publishing houses, although, as we shall see later, the possibilities for indies are growing.

Since the arrival of the digital revolution in publishing, experience has taught us that neither ebooks nor audio spell the death of print or of physical bookstores. Indeed the opposite is true. Continuing advances in production technologies for print books – whether POD or offset litho printed – mean it's now possible to repurpose the same intellectual property – your book – by publishing the same text in many formats. Even with a single type of book there are multiple variants – eg box sets of ebooks (either multiple or single author), different styles of print edition (colour, mono, illustrated, graphic, dyslexic, etc), hardback, paperback, commemorative edition – all within reach of the indie author. For a striking illustration, look up J K Rowling's Harry Potter books online and witness the many, many pages of product listings.

Back to Basics

However what has not changed very much is the lack of understanding and common ground between bookstores and self-published authors. Some self-published authors to give up on bookstores altogether, and some bookstores are known to have implemented a blanket ban on indie authors' books.

At ALLi, we have seen that, where booksellers and authors understand each other's needs and practices, there is a third way for indie authors and bookstores to work together for mutual benefit. This goes much further than simply stocking self-published books on their shelves.

This book is designed to help indie authors step back from the emotional debates and dramatic, headline-grabbing claims made by the press or inferred from the information (and often misinformation) on the internet. It provides context and background to facilitate open discussion and respectful, informed relationships between author and bookseller.

While many authors want to see their book in bookstores without fully understanding why—for example, because of a love of the stores, because of an assumption that's how books are sold—we encourage authors to step back and understand their own motives.

Don't let bookstore aspirations blind you to the opportunities you have to find your readers through other, equally good, if not more successful, distribution channels. Rather than "How can I get my book into a bookstore?," the first question you should ask is "How can I use my position as a self-publisher as an advantage to sell copies of my book?" For most indies, bookstore distribution is something to think about after you have already successfully sold books online, not before. The vast majority of indie authors make most of their income from online sales, and also enjoy their biggest margins there. Getting traction via ebook sales also allows indie authors to build their confidence, their reputation and their catalogue – all useful springboards for diversifying into print sales in bookstores and elsewhere.

The information and advice in these pages will help independent authors to approach bookstores confidently and competently, and to foster long-term relationships that will help both parties thrive in a spirit of cooperation and collaboration. And, though aimed at authors, it will help any bookseller who reads it to understand that good self-published books are an opportunity that can represent a useful additional income stream for their bookstore and a more direct connection with authors than is usual with trade-published authors.

Such creative and commercial opportunities are, of course, in the best interest of that most important person for all concerned: the reader.

2

TERMS OF REFERENCE
BOOKSTORES AND BOOKSELLERS

You say bookstore, I say bookshop. Before we get started, let's set some definitions. In publishing and the book trade, "bricks-and-mortar stores", or just "brick-stores" or, increasingly, "physical stores" are the terms most commonly used to refer to what the average book buyer calls a bookshop or bookstore. In publishing, we've got used to needing to differentiate between a physical retail outlet, as opposed to an online retailer.

Where British-English prevails, "bookshop" is more common than "bookstore" but for ease of reference, in this book physical stores are called **bookstores**, while those retailers who sell solely or mostly online are referred to as **online retailers**.

These days, bookstores almost always have an online presence too, with websites used to order books for home delivery and for click-and-collect orders, and perhaps blogs and social media accounts to attract online browsers to their stores.

The largest online book retailer is currently Amazon, (although other sites continue to increase their market share of ebooks and audiobooks, if not print). Many bookstores in many lands have long decried the impact the online giant has had on the physical trade sector. Complicating the situation, Amazon has since November 2015 demonstrated ambitions to embrace the physical bookstore market too, opening a trial bookstore in Seattle, Washington.

At the time of writing, it has added further physical stores differentiated into four brands: Amazon books, Amazon 4-star, Amazon go and Presented by Amazon (don't call the proofer, lower case for "books" and "go" is part of their brand identity).

Only the first two of these store chains carries books, and each also carries devices and merchandise. At time of writing they are trading solely in the USA, with 21 Amazon books stores across 13 states but you can keep up with the latest additions by doing a simple online search "find your Amazon physical book store".

While it's reasonable to expect the number of Amazon's physical bookstores to grow, it is not yet clear whether this will include territories beyond the USA, but for the foreseeable future we can expect its main revenue to be online. It's also important to remember that although Amazon started out with books, its offering continues to diversify. Therefore, in these pages, we will consider Amazon to be primarily an online retailer for now.

What Is an Independent Bookstore?

Bookstores fall within two broad categories: bookstore chains, in which a board of directors or other central body manages a group of stores, usually from a head office, in line with a consistent set of rules across all stores; and independents, or indie bookstores, which are one-off shops or very small chains.

Again, borderlines are blurry. The innovative and maverick James Daunt, MD of a large British chain of bookstores, Waterstones, has described himself as "an independent bookseller who just happens to be running a chain" (*The Bookseller*, 13 November 2015), because of the degree of autonomy, particularly in terms of ordering and merchandising, that he now allows at local level, which has resulted in the percentage of returns falling from 20% before he took over the chain, to an impressive 4%, leaving booksellers more time for interaction with customers rather than packing up unsold books to go back to their publishers. In the same article, which can be found through a search on the New York Times website, Tom Weldon, chief executive of Penguin Random House Books UK, backs up his claim, saying "He's essentially created a series of independent bookstores with the buying power of a chain." In 2019, the undauntable Daunt was also appointed chief executive of US chain Barnes & Noble, tasked with reversing its fortunes as he did for Waterstones. That's some juggling act.

While it's possible to be both a chain and independent of thought, when we talk about independent bookstores in this book, we mean the one-off shops. There are, though, a few indie bookstores with more than one branch. Just to complicate matters, Waterstones also owns a handful of bookstores that are not presented at members of its chain, with its distinctive black and white branding. Instead, they retain an independent, individual look, including their store names. "Harpenden Books, The Deal Bookshop, Blackheath Bookshop, Southwold Books and The Weybridge Bookshop are all owned by us but still trade 'Indie-Style'," says Connor Curran of Waterstones Customer Support. " We have also recently taken over the company 'Foyles' which is still trading under the old branding." In the ever more creative business of bookselling, nothing is straightforward.

We need to be clear here that when bookstores describe themselves as independent, they are not making a statement about how their stock is published. Although one might anticipate a natural affinity between independent bookstores and indie authors, seeing the word "indie" over the door of a bookstore does not mean they are more likely to stock self-published books than the most indie-resistant chain. Independent bookstores are not to be confused with the kind of bookstore that exists expressly to stock self-published books. That rare but interesting breed of retail outlet has different objectives and challenges, and is described in detail in Chapter 4, "Different Types of Bookstore."

Other Kinds of Stores That Sell Books

To further complicate matters, not all stores that sell books, on or offline, are bookstores. Depending on the kind of book you write, you may be keen to target specialist retailers whose customer profiles match that of your target reader.

Nonspecialist retailers selling books, sometimes called "special sales" in the trade, is another growing trend.

A small, carefully curated stock of books can perfectly supplement the ethos of a fashion or lifestyle brand. As in the old adage that "books furnish a room," the right mix of books can be used as a shorthand to demonstrate a shop's philosophy and character to the casual observer, such as Cordon Bleu recipe books in an upmarket kitchen shop, or style guides in a fashion retailer. These are considered as opportunities for indie authors separately in Chapter 4.

Booksellers Versus Bookstore Staff

I'll refer to the specialist staff who work in bookstores, i.e. the personnel who advise customers and take their money, as booksellers, rather than any of the other terms that are often used—sales advisers, shop assistants, counter staff, etc.

It's important to recognize that, in good bookstores, the staff are far more than just counter assistants ringing up sales, or *beepeuses* as the French so beautifully put it, the term named after the beeping sound of the supermarket checkout barcode scanner.

Unlike any online retailer's algorithm, a human bookseller in a bookstore will provide a personal response to any enquiry. I know a couple of booksellers whose first career was in medicine, and the process of matching a book to a customer is analogous to a doctor or nurse prescribing medication to cure a health issue. The subtleties of two-way human interaction are not likely to be matched by Amazon algorithms or any form of Artificial Intelligence (AI) any time soon.

A bookseller is a specialist who:

- cares about the market sector
- loves books and reading
- is hugely knowledgeable about reading trends and book news

- is passionate about uniting customers with books that will excite them.

Having such a person behind your book can make an enormous difference. If you're seeking to get your self-published books into bookstores, never underestimate the skills and importance of individual booksellers.

There is in any case a growing appetite for the more subtle, personal and satisfying bookstore experience among readers jaded with automatic recommendations online. In certain quarters, there's also a significant resistance to online purchasing of any kind.

Proprietors

All proprietors are likely to be booksellers, but not all booksellers are proprietors. Where I mean specifically a bookseller who owns an indie bookstore, I'll call them the proprietor. When I use the word "bookseller," on the other hand, I'll mean any customer-facing member of staff who works in the bookstore, which may or may not be the proprietor in an indie bookstore.

3

HOW BOOKSTORES OPERATE
WHAT INDIE AUTHORS NEED TO KNOW

At ALLi, we support the right of each indie author to choose how and where to market their book – but we also feel strongly that such decisions should be made for the right reasons from an informed standpoint. That is why, back in 2015, in the appropriate setting of a historic London bookstore's flagship premises (Foyles, Charing Cross Road), we made a presentation appealing to authors and bookstores to work together for mutual benefit. The principles we outlined then still hold true today.

We believe that indie authors whose books are published to professional standards (which ALLi encourages them to aim for) should feel comfortable and confident about presenting their books for consideration for sale in bookstores, should they wish to do so. One key purpose of this book is therefore to help indie authors navigate the right course to place their books in stores.

Many indie authors do not even consider trying to sell their books through bookstores:

- they prefer the simpler business model of ebook-only publishing
- they prefer the larger margin and lower production cost of

ebooks
- they publish print copies but have been unable to find a profitable means of selling them via bookstores
- they've tried it, but made a loss, due to the high margins expected by booksellers and the impact of sale or return losses
- they've been unable to persuade any bookstores to stock their books at any cost
- they haven't dared approach bookstores, for fear of a rebuff
- they assume bookstores don't stock self-published books on principle so don't bother asking.

The Author's Prerogative

At ALLi, we firmly believe that it is the author's prerogative to choose their own retail route, and there are no absolute rights and wrongs. Authors who sell well online, whether ebook only or also in print, may prefer to keep their working practices simple, and their profits optimal, by not venturing into physical bookstores. Print book distribution through bookstores is admin heavy and less admin means more time to write and sell books in easier ways i.e. through digital download.

There may be, however, many good reasons why an author prefers to sell solely through other means, such as online retail stores or hand-selling at events. But we want to ensure that every author has given bookstores due consideration and to give those authors who do decide to partner with bookstores confidence, through understanding their motivation for bookstore distribution, and the challenges in choosing that pathway.

Synergy with Bookstores

We also believe that there is a natural synergy between indie authors and indie bookstores, not only due to their obvious shared love of connecting readers with books, but in many other ways, as discussed in Chapter 10. If you don't want to take advantage of this synergy, that's up to you—but we don't want you for lack of information or inspiration to miss out on a growing range of exciting opportunities in bookstores.

Not Only for Indies

We believe that authors of all kinds, no matter how they are published, benefit from working closely with bookstores.

As a global organization representing indie authors, ALLi naturally focuses on the self-publishing sector. However, much of the content and principles of this guidebook is equally applicable to trade-published authors, many of whom are also less engaged than they might be with bookstores.

A Practical Collaboration

Authors and bookstores of all kinds and bookstores will work much effectively together if they can arrive at better mutual understanding and awareness, and by dispelling any nervousness about engaging with each other. To that end, this book provides not just a call to action, but also practical advice for authors such as:

- helpful insights into how bookstores operate
- advice on how to make your book bookstore ready
- guidelines on how to approach bookstores
- practical tips about the most effective supply chain for your needs
- inspiring case studies from authors working successfully with bookstores.

The Right Time

Why now? Over the past few years, there has been much reporting about the collective health of bookstores, but if as indie authors we work together with booksellers, we can only improve prospects for all of us. It's a complex picture, with very different scenarios around the world.

In some countries, the number of bookstores is on a healthy upward trend, whether or not bolstered by national pricing legislation that eliminates the undercutting of prices by bigger retailers that elsewhere threatens smaller traders. In others, there have been dramatic declines, whether steadily or sporadically, not only in bookstores, but across the spectrum of physical stores facing competition from online retailers, notably Amazon, Apple and Kobo.

Around the world, some commentators, in particular general media that always love a scaremongering story, have suggested that the decline of bookstores is inevitable, thanks to two parallel modern revolutions: the rise of online retailers and the emergence of ebooks. It's been relatively easy for reporters to field heartrending case studies of booksellers of forty years' standing having to close their store for lack of a buyer.

The press are also quick to embrace surveys undertaken by parties with a vested interest likely to skew the results, provided they make good headlines, and not only in stories regarding the book trade. These include surveys that indicate the plateauing or reduction of ebook sales, compared with print books. Drilling down into their source data reveals that they are leaving self-published ebooks out of the equation, as ALLi founder and director Orna Ross explained in her opinion piece SelfPublishingAdvice.org/ebook-sales-not-falling.

There have also been plenty of predictions that books are an endangered species, public appetite being diverted by the many other sources of entertainment and relaxation.

But the real situation is more encouraging. While some bookstores close, new bookstores are springing up, or old ones are being reinvigorated by exciting initiatives that fit them well to the needs of the twenty-first-century reader. Nic Bottomley, President of The Booksellers Association, said:

> In the UK, the trade is in its third consecutive year of growth in terms of bookshop numbers. Why did they fall before that? Books is where Amazon began, and it decimated the book buying market first. For some this was deservedly so, as they had become staid,

hobbyist shops. Those that remained are built around experiential service or extreme customer service. They are Amazon-proof.

The more successful chains are expanding, new players are entering the field, often from outside of the traditional bookstore arena, and the notion of a modern bookstore is fast evolving to become a more exciting, dynamic, and thriving arena.

Retail was ever thus. Business was ever thus. While it's true that many bookstores have closed, with plenty of neighborhoods losing their sole remaining bookstore, the same applies across many retail sectors—fashion, sports, household goods, etc. It would be astonishing if it were not so with booksellers trading patterns did not evolve from decade to decade.

Traders large and small come and go. Those who are able to read the signs of change in an ever-evolving marketplace stay ahead of the game. Those who are less farsighted or more conservative fall by the wayside.

Authors who recognize and embrace the change in bookstores will have the opportunity to form relationships with the successful traders, and to jump aboard their ship to sail into a brighter future.

If bookstores are evolving from old-style purveyors of books to multifaceted cultural centers celebrating reading and writing, it's great news for authors, especially those who embrace change opportunistically and who think outside the box. We'll be sharing a taster of such developments in Chapter 3.

A Broader Principle

Whatever lies ahead for bookstores, we believe that their continuing existence benefits all authors. If all authors support bookstores in as many ways as they are able, the stores' future will be brighter. As we'll see in Chapter 12, there are dozens of ways you can support bookstores, even if you choose not to sell your books via that route, and most of these ways won't cost you a penny.

Why should you do this? We believe the presence of bookstores in our shopping malls and on our main streets and our high streets, all around the world, helps create a richer cultural environment and fosters a love of books in society as a whole. We have therefore included:

- tips on other ways to work effectively with booksellers besides getting your books on their shelves
- easy ways to support bookstores at little or no cost.

ALLi's motivation isn't only to gain retail shelf space for self-published books and to help bookstores build profit for all parties. We also want to address the broader issue of ensuring indies are aware of the value to authors of visible, physical bookstores within our society and our communities.

Wherever you stand on the issues outlined above, we hope you will at least invest the small amount of time required to read this book. Then, if you still choose to give bookstores a wide berth, that's your right as an indie, and ALLi respects you for it.

If you're not already convinced that you want to be part of the bookstore scene, we hope you will be by the end of that section. But if not—well, that's your choice, and we support that too!

So, in short, this guidebook, *Your Book in Bookstores: ALLi's Guide to Print Book Distribution,* is being produced to help authors and bookstores work together for mutual benefit. It provides:

- a reality check on the feasibility of selling self-published books in bookstores,
- inside information to give you a better understanding of how bookstores operate,
- practical advice to help you do what it says on the cover—to sell your self-published books in bookstores—should you decide that's what you'd like to do

But before we go any further, let's set the context for our discussions, via an examination of what constitutes a bookstore, both historically and in the present, and what it might become in the future.

4

WHY BOTHER WITH BOOKSTORES?
THE BENEFITS OF PHYSICAL BOOKSELLING

Before you take the time and trouble to decide which bookstore to target, be sure you really want to get your books into bookstores. Why should you bother when plenty of indie authors, including some hugely successful and high-profile ones, ignore the sector, content with their online sales success?

Having already established their books and a following via online retailers, they are happy to stay in their groove of write, publish, repeat, as they watch their sales snowball. Many don't even stray beyond what is most people's entry point into self-publishing these days: publishing ebooks via KDP (Kindle Direct Publishing) to be sold through Amazon. However, as alternative ebook distribution platforms have grown and taken market share from Amazon, more authors are "going wide", as the jargon has it – and which is ALLi's recommended practice.

What is wide exactly? It means publishing your ebooks simultaneously on Rakuten Kobo, Nook, Apple Books, Tolino, and so on, either directly through those retailers' dashboards or via an aggregator such as Draft2Digital, PublishDrive, StreetLib or SmashWords. Publishing ebooks directly with each platform gives you certain advantages e.g. access to special promotions not available via aggregators – but there is a balance to be had between minimising labour and maximising marketing opportunities.

For comprehensive advice on how to choose the suppliers and services to help you go wide, see John Doppler's companion volume in this series, *Choose the Best Self-Publishing Services*.

Why Limit Yourself to Ebooks?

The reasons these authors cite for sticking to ebook only include:

- less time-consuming
- more profitable per book (typically 70% of selling price for Amazon ebooks priced $1.99–9.99)
- cheaper production costs—just a front cover jpeg and digital text, rather than a full wraparound cover with formatted interior
- no delivery costs
- frees up more time for writing more books and marketing the back catalog
- current customer base for ebooks provides adequate income
- anticipated sales of paperbacks would not generate sufficient profit to cover the additional production and marketing costs.

Why Invest in Print

Although a few bookstores promote ebook readers in-store, if you're ebook only, by definition, you are out of the running for getting your books stocked on physical bookshelves. ALLi therefore also recommends that you publish in print (and, as you become more established invest your author earnings back in audio too).

Robin Cutler, Director of IngramSpark, has long made the case for indie authors to include print in their catalog. She said:

Despite the publishing prophecies from five or so years ago claiming that readers were moving in mass to their ebook devices, we know that now and in the foreseeable future, the printed book continues to dominate the market as the preferred format for reading. The truth turned out to be that a huge number of people still prefer the experience of turning pages, browsing shelves of titles and carting around a reading device that hasn't changed much in the 1500 years since bound pages replaced the scrolls of antiquity.

As it turns out, there are some genres such as romance and thrillers where many readers prefer their content served up effortlessly and often for free to their iPad, Kindle or Kobo. But even now the most ardent advocates for digital publishing from a few years back are now suggesting that a multi-format strategy may be the best approach for indie authors today.

I have recommended for years that it's best for authors to make their content available in as many formats, and as widely available, as they can afford. With a publishing industry that is changing so rapidly, there is no way to predict an audience for your book or even know where and how readers prefer to purchase. With platforms such as IngramSpark that combine distribution directly with ebook and print-on-demand technology, this strategy is fairly easy and inexpensive to realize.

Even if you expect to sell most of your books in digital form – and most indie authors do still make the larger part of their income from ebooks – it is still worth having paperbacks so as to have something to "show and tell" at events, and to share with people who don't believe that books exist unless they see them in print, or who think ebooks don't count as actual books. Many indies who venture into print for the first time are surprised to find they sell more hard copies than they expected – although the rate does vary according to genre.

ALLi's recommendation is to publish your print books simultaneously on KDP Print and/or IngramSpark, which ensures consistent supply on both platforms. You must use the same ISBN on both, and wherever else you might choose to print the book, eg if you commission a small private print run, to avoid confusing the algorithms. If publishing across multiple platforms, you will need to buy your own ISBN, rather than using Amazon's free issue. This is worth doing in any case, because whoever owns a book's ISBN is deemed its publisher—more about the implications of ISBN choices in Chapter 7.

Equipped with a small stock at home for hand-selling and print-on-demand books available to order online, you open up the possibility of getting your book into bookstores.

A Different Business Model

Print generally has a much narrower potential for profit than ebooks. When you're selling print books online, the cost of order fulfilment is higher than for an ebook because it includes physical production and delivery – much more expensive than the delivery online of a digital ebook file.

When you sell your print books through a bookstore, not only do you have to cover the production costs, you're introducing an additional middleman – an intermediary with more substantial overheads than an online store: rent, staff, taxes, heating, lighting, advertising, etc.

Clearly these overheads have to be paid for, and that's why bookstores expect to receive a substantial discount on books they buy to sell on. Most booksellers will expect 35–45% from your recommended retail price, and even more for books for which they promise to provide extra sales support, for example 60% for books sold in high-volume outlets such as airport bookstores.

To many new indie authors, the need to factor in this extra level of costs comes as a shock, although it makes perfect sense. So why are we suggesting that authors should consider pursuing bookstore sales, when they stand to make even less profit than when selling print books online?

The Benefits of Bookstore Selling

Provided that you go into the prospect of selling through bookstores with realistic financial expectations—i.e. you may not make much profit or sell many copies—there are sound reasons for pursuing this path. Some of these are practical issues:

- Certain books are much harder to sell in digital format, in particular children's books, as younger readers still prefer to read print books.
- Very complex technical books full of diagrams, charts, photos, and other illustrations don't translate well into digital format.

There are also more emotional reasons for wanting to sell your books via bookstores:

- validation of your status as an author (in the same way that many successful indie authors would also be happy to accept a trade publishing contract, on the right terms, to indicate to themselves that they've really arrived as an author)
- personal love of bookstores as cultural centers in our society
- a love of physical books
- loyalty to specific bookstores where you are a regular customer
- a lifelong ambition to see your book on sale in a bookstore, formed long before ebooks and online book retailers took off, hard to shake off despite the book-retailing revolution that we've witnessed since the turn of the twenty-first century.

Piers Alexander, historical novelist, described on the ALLi blog his lasting passion for bookstores as the driving force behind his decision to focus the launch of his debut novel on a print edition with high production values with which to target bookstores.

Although it made his self-publishing process more complex and higher risk, as a serial entrepreneur he was happy to rise to the challenge. Piers said:

> I grew up in Luxembourg, and the best bit of visiting England as a kid was coming to bookstores with a sweaty pawful of pocket money. Booksellers are nice, thoughtful, helpful people, and their lives have become a lot more difficult in the age of the internet and book discounting. Even so, I frequently find them going out of their way to place books that they personally like, that they think their customers will like, rather than just going with the obvious bestsellers. When I decided to publish The Bitter Trade independently, I was very keen to get good reach through bookstores.
>
> The thing is, I like "proper books". I like holding them, infusing them with my own peculiar musk, and then passing them on to unsuspecting friends. And in an age when millions of writers are desperately trying to game the Amazon system, when quite ruthless email marketing companies drive everyone towards 99 cent ebook promotions, I love the fact that people pay good money for good books and find them in good bookstores. So I decided to print them in the old-fashioned way, which is a bit of a commitment.
>
> Going from 100 to 500 paperbacks halves the cost of production. Going to 2,000 plus halves it again—and you can't do that with print-on-demand. That means it's an all-or-nothing thing. I'm pleased to say that I broke even within seven months... until we print the next batch. Which is bigger! Ladies and gentlemen, don't try this at home. Stock control is a nightmare.
>
> And here's what happened: I've sold copies to I think about 10% of the UK's high street bookstores and libraries through the lovely people at Gardners, one of the UK's leading distributors. That's very cool. Even cooler is that the fiction buyer for WHSmith —who just loves historical novels—agreed to take a consignment for all their airport shops, and the book went into the charts...
>
> The best thing I ever did was to invest properly in print. I had a

dream of seeing The Bitter Trade in airports. My ex-agent thought of it as a literary novel, but I have always seen it as commercial. So I produced it in trade paperback format, took a deep breath and spent even more embossing and using spot UV (varnish) on the front cover—and cursed myself for a fool right up until the moment Matt Bates from WHS said that he liked the jacket, loved the story and could see it in his stores.

And by the way, most trade publishers have to pay a lot of money to get into the Airport Exclusives spots. I just had to print the books. I guess there's another lesson here: don't listen to people all the time. When it comes to the really big decisions, go with your gut.

Piers's strategy and determination were rewarded, but clearly also brought with them serious responsibilities and cost implications that are not to be taken lightly.

Scottish novelist Anne Stormont is another author whose love of bookstores dates back to her childhood, she said:

> I loved bookstores when I was little. My granny was the one who would take me and she would buy me books as an occasional treat. I still love them—the independents, the chains, the ones with coffee shops, galleries or gift shops attached—love them all. And although I do read in both ebook and paper format, I still prefer a proper paper book. I publish in both formats and I ask bookstores to stock my books. Long live the real books and long live the book shops.

These may be emotional reasons, but that doesn't invalidate them, especially when they are followed through with sound business decisions, as in the case of both authors quoted above.

Note the absence of one significant reason: to get rich. If it's the fast track to clear profit you're after, selling your books via bookstores is not the obvious route. For a start, you'll have to invest far more heavily to make your book bookstore-ready than simply to sell it online in ebook form. We'll talk more about that in Chapter 7, "How to Make Your Book Bookstore Ready."

But for all kinds of books, if you've invested the time and effort into producing a print book for hand-selling and promotional purposes, you might as well explore all retail opportunities, rather than just those to be found online. It would seem a shame not to at least investigate possibilities and options, so that you can make an informed decision about what would be in your own best interests.

If you're still reading this far, I'm assuming you've decided that you do want to try to get your books into bookstores, so the next step is to gain an understanding of exactly how bookstores operate, so that you can devise a campaign that will help you mesh with their practices and thus gain a greater chance of success.

5

PHYSICAL BOOKSTORES TODAY
PAST, PRESENT, AND FUTURE

F ew indie authors would disagree with the popular maxims "Self-publishing isn't a sprint, it's a marathon" or "We're in it for the long haul." But our self-governing status as author publishers makes us expect to be able to make things happen relatively quickly. We are used to acting fast on our decisions and implementing changes online that take effect almost immediately: uploading new books, changing metadata, switching prices prices.

However, when it comes to bookstores, we have neither that degree of control nor the speed of implementation at our disposal. Each author is only a tiny cog in the vast machinery of the bookstore retail ecosystem. To stand the best chance of success in getting our books stocked in bookstores, and to do so profitably, we need to understand they operate. We need to be able to view the bookstore from the bookseller's side of the counter.

Although the rate of change in the physical bookstore environment is less rapid than within its online equivalent, the nature of bookstores has changed substantially in our lifetime.

The Bookstore Past

You can find a long and fascinating history of the book trade in its various forms in Lewis Buzbee's *The Yellow-Lighted Bookshop*, but, for a bit of fun, let's start with an extract from an ALLi author's historical novel set in an eighteenth-century London bookstore. The joy of print-on-demand, which twenty-first-century authors take for granted, is put into perspective by this affectionate passage in Lucienne Boyce's novel *To The Fair Land* describing a chaotic scene from an era in which books were still handprinted by letterpress. To secure his copy of a bestseller by a mysterious anonymous author, the hero, Ben Dearlove, along with other would-be purchasers, has to wait while it is printed. The opening scene of Chapter 4 is reminiscent of a modern Black Friday superstore scuffle:

Who would have thought that book lovers could be so warlike? They jammed themselves around Mr Dowling's door, ignoring the fact that six people could not pass through a space wide enough for two, dealing out spiteful jabs and sly blows to one another. The stationer, watchmaker and music seller stood on their own doorsteps, complaining loudly about the crowd that made it impossible for their customers to pass.

Ben Dearlove comes to the rescue of the besieged bookseller, Mr Dowling. On reaching the front of the queue, he ducked down and crawled under the girl's skirts, at which she set up a greater shrieking than ever. Emerging on the other side of her lumpy knees, he slithered under the table, struggled to his feet, snatched *An Account of a Voyage to the Fair Land* from His Lordship's footman and clambered onto the table.

"Ladies and Gentlemen!" he bellowed. "If you have a ticket, please wait on this side of the shop. If you have not yet put your name down for a copy, please move to the right and Sam will come round and make a note of your details. Tickets only on this side... Yes, sir, every printing machine between here and London Wall is rattling off copies as we speak... No, madam, to the right if you wish to put your name down."

"Mr Dearlove!" Dowling gazed up at the young man in grateful surprise. "Thank heaven! I did not think I could withstand the siege much longer!"

While delivery from publisher to reader became less fraught in time, particularly with the coming of the railways, the supply chain remained, until recently, dictated by publishers and their printing schedules. This included the control of selling prices. Minimum prices of books were determined by publishing houses, and in many countries book prices were protected against discounting by law. (In many countries they still are, preventing the erosion of publishers' profits and therefore, in theory at least, author earnings.) Each new book had to be printed in large quantities, typically high hundreds and even thousands, to arrive at a marketable unit cost. Part of the publisher's responsibility was to warehouse inventory to be called off as required by individual bookstores.

Until the 1930s, books were sold almost exclusively in bookstores, in hardback, on the publishers' terms, at relatively high prices. Buying books was considered a luxury, and lending libraries the only means for many people to obtain books to enjoy at home.

Then came the paperback revolution in the 1930s, fueled by Allen Lane, founder of Penguin Books, who was seeking a way of putting high-quality but affordable paperbacks into the hands of the masses for the equivalent price of a packet of cigarettes.

In the fortunate position of having prices protected from competition, booksellers could stock books safe in the knowledge that no one could buy them elsewhere at a lower cost. There were also some subscription services by post, offering club editions of books, but these were of limited lists of club editions not available in stores.

Toward the end of the twentieth century, in some countries, such a restrictive practice had started to be regarded as more of an unfair cartel, mitigating against the end user, the reader, in order to protect all other parties in the deal. It was therefore removed.

This freed bookstores to compete against each other on price, which particularly benefited the new bookstore chains that rose up in the late twentieth century. However, it also caused the sector to be targeted by much larger players in retailing, such as vast grocery superstore chains, luring book buyers away from traditional stores, at least for the very limited list that they deign to stock in the relatively small amount of shelf space designated for books.

More threatening still, in the case of online book retailers, with unlimited virtual shelf space, bookstores faced competition across their range, at least in terms of stock, if not customer service. While price protection was in place, the bookseller's main concern was to curate appropriate stock for local clientele, run the store efficiently, and treat customers well enough to make them want to patronize that store rather than anyone else's.

After all, customers had no alternative, other than to defect to a different bookstore or to borrow the book from their public library. If you wanted to buy a book, you went to a bookstore. If the bookseller was obliging and knowledgeable, well and good. If not, in the pre-internet age, when you couldn't "Google a book" or look it up in seconds on Amazon, finding a chosen title could be a challenge.

The circumstances that book buyers would put up with in order to buy their books were remarkable by today's standards. An example is Foyles' legendary Charing Cross Road store, then set in a rabbit warren of a building (across two buildings, in fact), where books were generally displayed by publisher rather than genre. When you did find one you wanted to buy, you had to visit two separate service counters in different places in the store to secure your purchase.

Even so, customers adored the shop and were hugely loyal.

My mother used to work there in the 1950s, and when I described to her the wonderful new flagship store, designed in consultation with customers to make a highly enjoyable shopping experience, she said, "That's a shame. I rather liked the old way!" She tells a captivating story of how even staff discounts were arrived at erratically. Each Friday, staff presented their choice of books to the store's director, the elderly Miss Christina Foyle, who decided on an individual basis what discount each person should receive.

Interestingly, some of the most innovative new stores are now making a point of difference of sorting and displaying their books in unconventional categories, to add an element of excitement and surprise for browsers.

In those days, bookselling was perceived almost as a profession, and the bookseller respected as a knowledgeable and well-read cultural adviser. In his introduction to Penelope Fitzgerald's poignant novel *The Bookshop*, set in the 1950s, novelist David Nicholls recalls:

> For several years in the mid-1990s, I worked in a West London bookshop... My colleagues for the most part were English Literature graduates or postgraduates, knowledgeable and passionate about the written word. Yes, we were shop assistants but the fact that we sold books, as opposed to socks or potatoes or saucepans, gave the job a certain respectability, kudos almost... Books mattered, they were different, they were improving.

The Bookstore Present

Fast forward to the twenty-first century, and the trading context for the average bookstore is very different.

In countries that still have fixed pricing for books, bookstores continue to enjoy greater stability.

"In France, all new books are sold a the same price, regardless of whether it's online or a local bookstore," reports Andy Bromley of IngramSpark. "Many English-speaking markets are finding it tough and I suspect Australia will find it difficult in the coming years, due to the way the online bookstores are gearing up."

However in many countries, publishers are no longer able to fix prices and may even be forbidden by law to do so.

The impact of free market pricing on bookstores and authors can be harsh. For example, where publishers negotiate with chain stores to produce special editions of cherry-picked bestsellers to retail at bargain prices in grocery superstores, the margin for authors can be almost nil.

(One ALLi member reports that his trade publisher's deal to supply 10,000 copies of a book to a grocery chain yielded him just $250 in royalties.) In some ways, price cutting in non-bookstores is as invidious at threat to bookstores as competition from Amazon.

The size, structure, and setup of stores in general has changed radically during living memory. Whereas once all bookstores were in a city, town or village setting, the rise of out-of-town shopping malls has fostered the growth of bigger stores, with more staff, a broader stock, and a larger clientele drawn from a wider catchment area.

Smaller bookstores in town-centre settings find it easier to position themselves as important players in the local community, getting involved in neighbourhood events and building relationships with local schools, book groups and authors. When I visit the small indie booksellers near me, I'm greeted by name the minute I enter the door, and I have long and interesting conversations with the single staff member who is usually on duty. That is a great starting point for building a relationship – and for booksellers to hand-sell books they think are right for you as a customer.

Many bookstores, large and small, try to engage with customers by offering loyalty schemes to encourage return visits. While such schemes can also provide valuable data about individual's buying habits, it is much harder for physical stores – impossible, actually – to tailor each customer's visit to reflect their past buying habits. There is no physical of equivalent of showing personalised recommendations to each individual shopper.

With growing online competition, large chains must keep costs under tight control to keep their businesses viable. Staff budgets have been particularly vulnerable, and in some stores this has meant pegging staff pay, and reducing shop floor staff numbers and training costs. But in a good bookstore, customers won't mind having to stand in line to to consult a professional bookseller, because they value the personal connection and what Nic Bottomley describes as "extreme customer service".

There are, of course, lots of good things about these bigger stores that enhance the customer experience: more space for a much greater product range, including diversification into nonbook products such as stationery and gifts (not least because they can carry higher profit margins); coffee shops; browsing areas with comfy sofas; event areas; and, in countries where there is no fixed pricing, special offers that are negotiated with publishers, such as 3-for-2 offers and large discounting. Publishers also often buy guaranteed display space in high-traffic areas such as tabletops or outward-facing prime spot shelves. While this is an income stream not usually available to independent bookstores, most indie booksellers would not welcome paid product placement, valuing their freedom of choice and priding themselves on curating their own stock.

The Impact of Online Book Retailers

The impact of online book retailers like Amazon, Flipkart, and The Book Depository on the fortunes of traditional bookstores is obvious. Big-box book retailers like Barnes & Noble in the US, Chapters in Canada, and Dymocks in Australia may have once driven small, independent booksellers out of business, but today in the shadow of ebooks and online retail, even megachains are suffering.

Online retailers have provided a convenient alternative for a public that spends an ever-increasing amount of time online in the comfort of their own home or workplace. They make it easier to browse stock at any time of day or night, because these stores are not hampered by opening and closing times, or the need to shut the doors at night to vacuum the carpets and replenish the bookshelves. They make it relatively easy to find the book you're looking for, or to suggest titles on the subject that you are seeking if you don't have a specific book in mind, (though less sensitively than if done by human advisers), using carefully calculated algorithms, bolstered by analytical data of what is currently selling well.

They also make impulse purchases more tempting by flagging up to readers what else they might like based on their current or previous orders. Bookstores cannot compete with that: their counters by the till may be stocked with high-margin impulse extra buys such as bookmarks and stationery, but these don't change to match each customer's historic buying pattern.

Not only do online retailers tempt the browser with clever arrays of appropriate products, they also, most importantly, cut prices. Special offers may even be set up without the publisher or self-published author's knowledge. The price cuts on new launches of likely bestsellers, such as much-heralded celebrity autobiographies or the next big blockbuster from a top fiction author, will often be reduced beyond what conventional bookstores might offer. Amazon can afford to do this simply because it is confident that it will sell such vast numbers. (It's the same economy of scale that enables those companies that bring round little catalogs to places of work, listing a very small number of new and top-selling books at much reduced prices.)

Amazon's pricing policy has created an expectation among the book-buying public and Amazon fans that it's always worth looking on Amazon before making a bookstore purchase, because it's likely to be cheaper there than elsewhere. Those who subscribe to the Amazon Prime service don't even have to factor in delivery costs. The customer perception is that delivery is free, because Prime is a one-off annual charge. Amazon has also increased its appeal by bundling a growing number of services into the Prime offer, including music and video streaming,

Hence the rise of that accursed practice, show-rooming. There are few bookstore staff who have not experienced the aggravation of helping a customer with an enquiry about a specific book, only to be told by the customer, "Thanks very much, I'll order it on Amazon when I get home. It's cheaper." Some customers even have the temerity to scan the QR code or barcode on the book proffered by the bookseller and order it online in front of the bookseller's eyes, not realising the implications for their business. It's as if they assume all book retailers are part of one big happy family with the publishers and the authors, all of whom will get their fair share of the takings at the end of the day out of one giant pot of money. Oh, if only...

Many traditional bookstore chains have started to offer online stores of their own, to help fight back against the onslaught of online specialists. Some offer the best of both worlds; for example, a click-and-collect service, grocery store style, so that customers may order their books and collect at their own convenience. For those who are out at work all day, Amazon's home delivery service is not necessarily ideal, hence Amazon's establishment of a growing number of community collection points.

While online book retailing continues to be a threat to bookstores, it would be simplistic to give them sole responsibility for any bookstore closures.

Firstly, physical stores of all kinds have faced tough trading times in recent years. Many big-name retail chains have gone under, including some that seemed indestructible, with enormous brand loyalty. All stores face similar threats: the growing costs of trading (ever-increasing rents, rates and staff wages), coupled with the increasing popularity of buying online.

Local population patterns change. For example, some formerly thriving city-center shopping areas have become ghost towns as out-of-town malls have grown up. On the plus side, other formerly derelict areas have been revived by redevelopment programs. For instance, many disused harbors and dock areas have been transformed into fashionable, desirable communities for the affluent, often including upmarket retail areas that may house new bookstores.

All round the world, a large part of the highest-value, highest-margin segments of the business, such as hardback fiction, are steadily migrating to ebook and online fulfillment.

However, rumours of the decline of bookstore numbers are misleading, as this report from the American Booksellers Association website explains:

> Over the past 10 years, there has been a national resurgence for independent bookstores. Nationally, new stores are opening, established stores are finding new owners, and a new generation is coming into the business as both owner/managers and frontline booksellers. For the ninth year in a row ABA bookstore membership has grown, with stores operating in more than 2,400 locations.

This represents an astonishing 38% growth in number of locations between 2011 and 2019.

And, importantly, as a channel, independent bookstore sales are up. Overall book sales across indie bookstores for 2017 increased 2.6 percent over 2016, with a compound annual growth rate of 5.4 percent over the past five years. And so far for 2018, sales in the indie channel are up approximately 5 percent over 2017. All of this is a result of the fact that indie booksellers remain a resilient and entrepreneurial group — and that independent bookstores offer a unique — and unparalleled — opportunity for the discovery of new authors and great writing. While not every bookstore or community has seen this growth, the national trends are clear. Because indie stores have vital and unique ties to their communities they serve as important community centers, connecting readers and book buyers more closely with authors, great writing, other passionate readers, and their neighbors.

This is especially encouraging because it is happening in such a geographically vast territory, in which many occupants live too far from bookstores to be regular customers and therefore buy books online by default.

Similarly in the UK, in 2019 bookstore numbers are in their third successive year of growth. Says Nic Bottomley, "While some stores closed, deservedly so as they had become staid, hobbyist shops, those that remain are more Amazon-proof, built around experiential service or extreme customer service."

Some businesses that have been floundering for years have turned themselves around and returned to profit, with heavily revised business models to suit modern market demands. The British chain Waterstones, once heading the same way as Barnes & Noble, is now comfortably in profit, and its chief executive, James Daunt, is slated to improve the fortunes also of Barnes & Noble, to which he has also been appointed CEO.

Some chains have been extending their reach with new branches and ambitious expansion plans. Announcements of new bookstores opening abound. Many chains are expanding, and numerous new indies are entering the market, often bringing with them valuable experience from previous careers in other sectors such as law or medicine. The Suffolk Anthology, in Cheltenham, England, launched by medical doctor, Helene Hewett, was profitable in its first year, thanks to her careful research of the marketplace, mentoring from other indie booksellers, and her gently prescriptive approach to hand selling.

"Running an independent bookstore these days is much more about being part of the community than just selling books," she says. Her focus on building relationships with both local writers and readers is paying off. She is an enthusiastic host to the monthly authors group I run there, and every time I visit, the appreciation and loyalty of her local clientele is palpable. I witnessed her prescribe the best books to meet a gentleman's request for his grandchildren, before he turned to me to say completely spontaneously, "We are so lucky to have such a great service here for our community."

Equally, small independents have ridden the storm by rejigging their stock and expanding their offer with a careful selection of non-book items, appealing events programs, and promotions. In the US, the American Booksellers Association's highly successful US IndieBound campaign encourages readers to "Cultivate Community – Shop Local", while the UK's Booksellers Association's high-profile "Books Are My Bag" campaign is now a popular annual fixture.

While no bookstore has customer data as detailed or as extensive as Amazon's, they know what sells through their own tills. Booksellers order stock to match their specific clientele, whom they know and have chatted to in person, rather than just by analyzing historic buying patterns.

Bookstores also have certain elements unique to their business model that other physical retailers might envy.

The Sale or Return Advantage

Firstly, there is generally a sale or return deal with publishers, which means that any books that do not sell after a set period of time can be returned to the supplier for full credit.

"Sale or return is the reason most book stores exist," observes ALLi partner member Laurence O'Bryan. "They are showrooms for the product of traditional publishers who can pay for returns because of the sales of their blockbuster books. This model, with all the freight and high levels of returns for most books is fundamentally uneconomic and environmentally wasteful. One UK pulping plant handles 25 million books a year. Expecting indie authors, trying to be green, to support this shockingly wasteful model, is not financially or environmentally sustainable."

There is an important proviso to the sale or return model, says Peter Snell, who for many years ran the highly successful Bartons Bookshop in Leatherhead, UK. "They must be in pristine condition, and up to a ceiling of 10% of the total order from the distributor, or 50% for event orders."

This is to guard against irresponsible or unrealistic ordering habits. "It's wrong to have an industry built around over-buying and pulping," says Nic Bottomley. "The Booksellers Association is seeking an alternative model to avoid excess books being shipped around only to be destroyed."

In any case, most booksellers would rather sell the books than return them, because while they don't lose money by returning unsold books, nor do they make any. Every return means that they've had that part of a shelf tied up with a nonpaying lodger. It's also time-consuming to remove books from the shelves and package them up to return to the supplier. A further deterrent is the knowledge that their ultimate destination on return is likely to be either a cut-price remainder bookstore or a pulping plant, on the assumption that returned books. Often they do not even have to return the whole book, just the barcode or front cover, to prove it's not been sold – an act of destruction that goes against the grain for any book lover.

Just-in-Time Delivery

Secondly, the book trade generally practices just-in-time delivery for books that are in stock at the publisher's warehouse. This allows for optimal use of shelf-space in-store, while also offering a valuable service to bookstore customers: speedy delivery of special orders.

The business model of the Big Five and plenty of small publishers is still to print in large quantities and hold large inventory to be called off by customers as required. When customers order a book available from their usual distributor, bookstores usually receive next-day delivery, at a speed of service that matches Amazon's, but without charging the customer for postage. All the customer needs to do is call back into the store at their convenience to collect the purchase. This is a good fit with the modern click-and-collect mentality, although the bookstore special order model has been around for a lot longer than Amazon.

Because most self-published authors avoid the need to hold inventory by using print-on-demand (POD) services, orders for their books will take a little longer. Self-publishing print books simultaneously via IngramSpark and KDP Print (ALLi's strong recommendation, see Chapter 7) will ensure that bookstores can order your books via their usual distributor, whose database is partly fed by IngramSpark's catalogue.

And here's a note of encouragement for any indie author who cannot secure permanent shelf-space in-store for their books. Look behind the trade counter in any bookstore and you will see a large quantity of special orders awaiting collection by customers. A substantial proportion of the books sold via bookstores are one-off orders, rather than stocked in the main store. Peter Snell estimates 30-40% of his daily sales were of special orders. This is encouraging evidence that customers will speak up to request books that aren't in stock, and that booksellers are willing to go to the trouble to order them in – after all, these are guaranteed sales that will never need to be returned. We'll return to this topic in a later chapter ("Other Ways of Selling Books In-store").

Bookstores Yet to Come

While it would be foolhardy to predict how many bookstores will be trading in five years' time, or ten or twenty, given current trends, it seems certain that, despite online traders' ambitions and successes, there will still be plenty of trading to be done—and enough to be worth any self-respecting self-publishing author's while to consider them a significant target as a means of connecting with the book-buying public. New players will enter, playing to their own special strengths. Future bookstores are likely to be much more than bookselling zones, offering added value to the customer through a program of community events and services, meeting local social needs on a wider level. Whether or not it can be done at a profit is another matter, and in Chapter 5 we'll help you decide whether you should be targeting these bookstores with your books, before going on to equip you to do it as efficiently and cost-effectively as possible. But first, let's drill down a little further into the nature of bookstores, and of other stores that sell books without necessarily being dedicated bookstores, to help you choose which shops to target.

For More Insight into the Bookseller's Mindset

In the meantime, if this chapter has made you want to know more about the bookseller's point of view, you might also like to do the following:

- read booksellers' memoirs
- read novels set in bookstores and/or written by authors with bookselling experience (you'll find a recommended further reading list in the Appendix of this book)
- go to work in a bookstore as an intern, temp or part-time assistant
- befriend and chat to your local bookseller, asking questions about the business (just be careful to pick a time when the store is quiet so as not to affect trade)
- watch comedy classics such as the TV series *Black Books* or the bookstore sketch in Marty Feldman's "Marty Amok" show (easy to find on YouTube – search for "Marty Amok bookseller")
- watch movies set in bookstores such as *Notting Hill* and *You've Got Mail*

6

DIFFERENT TYPES OF BOOKSTORE
CHAINS INDIES & OTHER OUTLETS

It's all too easy, in our fervor to get our books into bookstores, to make insufficient allowance for their differences. This chapter outlines different types of bookstores and determines how best to approach each type.

Bookstore Chains

Obviously stores in big chains will have a different ethos from the small independents. Whether the chain is growing or shrinking, they will usually have strong corporate branding and company policies composed in a distant head office.

If I took you blindfolded into any branch of the British chain Waterstones, for example, as soon as you were unmasked, you'd know at a glance that you were in a Waterstones store, with its distinctive windowless rooms, black bookshelves and folksy shelf-edgers with handwritten personal reading recommendations from their staff . Even though their geographical locations may be wildly different, once you've walked through the entrance, you're unmistakably on Planet Waterstones. My nearest branch, in an enclosed out-of-town shopping mall near Bristol, has a bland view of a walkway and other shop fronts, whereas the one I visited on holiday in Oban on the northwest coast of Scotland has a stunning harbor view at the starting point of a voyage to the Outer Hebrides.

For chains, buying will be done centrally, and buying policy will be dictated centrally, but the stores would be less profitable and successful if they held exactly the same stock in every branch, regardless of the local demographic and geography. Even within a large chain, there will be some obvious local variations, particularly in stock ordering. In the Oban store, for example, there is an abundance of books about Scottish interests and the Highlands and Islands, whereas in the Bristol store nearest me the local interest books are all about Bristol. Yet their shared corporate identity is clear.

The situation is analogous to grocery retailing: the same chain that stocks caviar and top-price champagne in an upmarket area will stock cheap white sliced bread and cut-price lager in a less well-to-do area, all under the same recognisable branding.

The image of the bad corporate chain stores gobbling up brave little independents was crystallized in the 1998 Nora Ephron film *You've Got Mail*, in which the heroine, played by Meg Ryan, runs a venerable children's bookshop in Manhattan, a nurturing, warm-and-fuzzy, personal-services kind of place, while the tainted hero, played by Tom Hanks, is the lowbrow owner of a chain of superstores intent on putting her out of business.

Your stores are "big, impersonal, overstocked, and full of ignorant salespeople," she tells him, a sentiment you still hear widely stated in the book world. But actually large stores are making more risky and experimental fiction, more first novels, and more serious nonfiction available to general readers than ever before.

"The book business was an elitist, standoffish institution," Len Riggio told *BusinessWeek* in 1998. "I liberated it from that."

Riggio is the retailing entrepreneur who launched the Barnes & Noble superstore concept, with in-store coffee shops and spacious reading alcoves, that spread to Borders and Books-A-Million, and then to chains and independents the world over, turning the then rarified and elitist world of bookstores into recreational experiences.

"Riggio's critics have mocked his populist pose," says cultural commentator Brooke Allen, writing in *The Atlantic*, "but it should be taken seriously". Brooke said:

Before the appearance of the chains, a relatively highbrow, urban clientele shopped at the independents, and a relatively lowbrow, largely regional one bought mass-market titles at supermarkets, price clubs, and drugstores. Now, thanks to the chains and to internet sales, the vast territory between the two extremes has been bridged.

Elitists may carp, but the truth is that they are no longer quite so elite. These days shoppers in Buford, Georgia, and Rapid City, South Dakota, can pick up important titles such as Norman Cantor's Inventing the Middle Ages, Eugene Genovese's Roll, Jordan, Roll, and Andrew Motion's biography of John Keats—titles that are neither "popular" nor newly published—at their local Borders. (None of these books were available at the venerated independent Manhattan bookstores St Marks Bookshop and Three Lives, or at Los Angeles's hip and highbrow Book Soup, when I called.)

The reality is that big chains and small indie bookstores can comfortably co-exist and that there is room for both. Occasionally a chain buys up an indie but keeps its branding. In the UK Waterstones now owns the highly prestigious Hatchards bookshop in the heart of London's affluent Piccadilly (official bookseller to Her Majesty the Queen, HRH Prince Philip and HRH Prince Charles, no less), but has retained its character and branding. More recently it acquired the vibrant chain Foyles, bringing new efficiencies to operations through its economy of scale, without changing the look or feel of the store.

Waterstones has also added a new strand to its offering: stores that are individually designed to match the local vernacular, trading under a quasi-independent name, and designed to look as if they are one-off independents, such as Harpenden Books, The Deal Bookshop,

Blackheath Bookshop, Southwold Books and the Weybridge Bookshop. They are all owned by Waterstones but trade in their own style.

There is no real subterfuge. The Waterstones ownership is still clearly visible if you look for it, though there was a bit of an outcry by some who felt they'd been hoodwinked, but actually it's the same strategy that has worked very well in other sectors. For example, pub or restaurant chains that run to a precise, successful formula but with no two venues looking alike.

The big chains of bookstores are likely to have centralised buying policies. Lots of indie authors have said to me that they've been told by the local branch of a bookstore chain that it's company policy not to stock self-published books. They tell author friends the same thing, and before you know it, it's accepted as a universal truth.

If you have approached a bookstore and been turned down with that line, it's very likely that either (a) the staff member is misinformed about corporate policy, (b) they can tell at a glance that your book isn't viable for their store and they think this is the kindest way of rejecting you, or (c) you've really rubbed them up the wrong way and they don't want to deal with you under any circumstances. We'll come on to how to make a more effective approach in Chapter 8, "How to Pitch Your Book to a Bookstore."

The fact is, bookstore chains can and do stock self-published books —provided they are approached in the right way and that they are convinced that your book will earn them money. (You'll find some inspiring case studies in Chapter 11.)

Independent Bookstores

Indie stores have much greater freedom to curate their stock in line with their own preferences and, most importantly, their customers'.

It's often the quirkiness of small indie shops and their projection of the owner's personality that makes them so alluring. Indeed, it would be hard to find any two independent bookstores that could be mistaken for being part of the same chain. For a whistle-stop tour indicating the enormous range to be found within the independent bookstore sector, check out Jen Campbell's *The Bookshop Book*, which profiles dozens of bookstores from all around the world, punctuated by interviews with famous authors talking about their fans.

Independent booksellers, like indie authors, relish their freedom and independence. They're often founded and staffed by people who have worked for the bookstore chains, so they are highly experienced. They find it refreshing to no longer have to adhere to corporate guidelines dictated from remote head offices with shareholders to please.

Booksellers in independent stores are closer to the impact of the bottom line than employees in big stores. The proprietor of a small indie store not only depends on its success for a salary, but might also be using the family home to guarantee the business, and so stand to lose the house if the business folds. They are also responsible not just for keeping the store stocked and the customers happy, but for all the management tasks that would normally be shared between the large staff of a corporation: financial management and planning, tax returns, marketing, personnel management, property maintenance. Just as we self-published authors must take responsibility for the full job range of a publisher, the independent bookstore proprietor is CEO, personnel manager, finance officer, stock controller, and so on. Selling books to customers may be what drives the business, but it's a tiny part of what the proprietor actually does.

To be a successful independent bookseller, you have to be an entrepreneur, a multitasker, and an independent thinker. That makes them more accessible than suited executives tucked away in remote corporate HQs—but that doesn't make them fair game to buttonhole at any time.It's also their prerogative to decide at local level whether or not to stock self-published books – but at least when you visit an indie store, you're quite likely to be served by the proprietor, or at least be able to meet him in-store to make your pitch. Careful planning of your approach will improve your chances of success. We'll discuss strategies and tactics in future chapters.

Specialist Bookstores

The interests and constraints of bookstores, whether part of a chain or independent one-offs, will be dictated and constrained by two factors: their degree of specialism and their location.

Particularly if you're writing nonfiction, you should seek out any specialist bookstores for which your books would be a perfect match. For example, in the UK, Stanfords supplies travel-related books and maps, so if you've self-published a memoir of how you circumnavigated the world on a unicycle, it'll be an obvious target, because a greater proportion of space will be given over to travel-related books, and its customers shop there specifically because they're interested in travel. If you arrive in the store on your unicycle, you'll gain credibility and interest!

Specialist bookstores may cluster near relevant locations. Expect to find a medical bookstore on the campus of a medical school, or a legal bookstore near law courts and lawyers' chambers. They're worth seeking out if your book's the right match—but equally, you can save yourself some pain if you don't bother asking in a cookery specialist bookstore whether they'd like to take your latest zombie vampire novel.

Indie author Yvonne Payne has sought out a most appropriate specialist store for her historical novel set in Crete:

> *Kritsotopoula, Girl of Kritsa* has its basis in a true story set in our home village of Kritsa on the Greek island of Crete. In the nearby holiday resort of Elounda, the wonderful Eklektos Bookstore is popular with locals and holidaymakers alike. I decided that, if the owner of Eklektos, Lynne McDonald, read my draft novel and agreed to stock it as a paperback, I would go ahead with publication. Not only did Lynne agree to stock the book but she also acts as my distributor to get the books into Crete. We now take every opportunity to give each other support, knowing that what is good for one of us is good for the other.

Check out secondhand bookstores, many of which also carry new books, aiming to get the best of both worlds by diversifying. Conversely, some bookstores that have previously sold only new stock now supplement their new book business with secondhand or rare book sections that can also operate online, bringing in another income stream.

Indie-Only Bookstores

One relatively new form of specialism is to stock only books published by small independent presses or self-published authors. A number of retailers offer this service online, sometimes as an offshoot of an organization associated with indie authors, with obvious vested interests, such as:

- publishing services companies that have helped the authors concerned self-publish their books
- book evaluation services
- book award schemes

There are also a handful of bricks-and-mortar bookstores that are attempting to do the same in physical form for purely philosophical reasons. This is a bold and interesting business model, because it's not strictly customer focused. The average reader doesn't choose books on the basis of who publishes them, or whether they are self-published or trade-published. Most people, if challenged, would be unable to tell you the name of the publisher of the last book they read. Many wouldn't understand the difference between self- and trade-published, and fewer still would care about it. They're simply looking for good books produced to professional standards.

Buying indie books is not really comparable to choosing to buy fair trade products, for example, or organically produced food, or clothing ethically produced without exploitation of child labor. If stores were to look for books that were produced at a living wage, most books would be ruled out altogether, including trade-published ones!

While we can't help empathising with the notion of wanting to support indie authors, we acknowledge the skill and care required to make this business model work. The success of such shops depends on as careful curation as any other community-based bookstore. If by definition you are ruling out all trade-published books by definition, you need to offer an exceptionally appealing customer experience in other ways. Either that, or you need to set up some kind of partnership with indie authors so that they are investing in your business, e.g. through a shelf rental agreement, common in stores selling handicrafts.

One example was Florida bookstore PJ Boox, run by Patti Brassard Jefferson for several years before ceasing trading in 2019. Her point of difference was the strategy of displaying all its books face out, giving each author a floating wall shelf on which to showcase their books, in return for a small fee, and offering the shopper an aesthetically pleasing and unusual shopping experience. She also scheduled author events, facilitating video chat options for featured authors too far away to visit in person. "Being able to connect authors and readers directly takes the entire book experience to a different level," says Patti. "Today's readers don't always want to be told what to read. They are discovering new authors of their own. We just make that quest easier."

Other bookstores have experimented with this model, but indie authors can be reluctant to effectively subsidise a bookstore by renting shelf-space, not least because POD printed books have a higher unit cost and therefore they have a narrower profit margin for both author and bookseller. An alternative for indies wishing to pursue this route is to invest in a large private print run for direct sales, thus opening up a bigger margin – more on this idea later.

If you are able to squeeze enough profit for both parties out of this model, you might feel that indie-only bookstores would be a natural fit for your self-published books. On the other hand, you might worry that such bookstores might seem to ghettoize indie books when it's more in our collective interest to gain parity for them and see them lined up on the same shelves together. You decide, because, hey, you're independent.

See ALLi's #OUTIA (Open Up To Indie Authors) campaign for more on this. Allianceindependentauthors.org/open-up-campaign).

In parallel, some online retailers offer indie-only books on principle, but the average reader will need a good reason to seek those out, rather than plumping for the websites of the bigger, general online retailers, or the website of their favorite bookstore. Although indie authors tend to be mutually supportive, buying and reading each others' books, general readers are usually no more intent on buying only indie books than only books with blue covers or written only by authors whose names include the letter Z. What readers want is a good book, and the success or failure of any book-retailing enterprise depends upon the bookseller's ability to curate what the target readers want.

In January 2020, an alternative model was launched by entrepreneur and publisher Andy Hunter, in collaboration with the American Booksellers Association and Ingram. With a small staff, he launched Bookshop (bookshop.org), a site that will offer indie bookstores, authors, and publishers a way to competitively sell their books online, with a link to a point of purchase that excludes Amazon. He aims to match Amazon's strategy and customer service while helping traditional stores survive.

It's too soon to judge how successful this new approach might be, but ALLi Watchdog John Doppler comments:

> Persuading authors and booksellers isn't the hard part: it's persuading the readers to change their buying habits, use an unfamiliar retailer, and forgo the benefits Amazon offers (free shipping, one-stop shopping, easy returns, unparalleled selection, copious reviews, etc.).

Time will tell.

Unusual Bookstores

You find bookstores in the most surprising places. Fun photos of bookstores housed on rickshaws, tricycles, houseboats, and even donkeys abound on the internet – travelling bookshops with a constantly varying target audience. There are bookstores in converted chapels and churches, in disused barns and manor houses. Just about any building or vehicle can be adapted to house a bookstore, with the addition of shelves and a till. A quirky or romantic setting will add to the charm for the customer, though not always for the staff, who must try to provide efficient customer service without the benefits of modern technology or architecture. The nature of the location may impact their choice of stock and their capacity, making curation particularly challenging. There are only so many books you can fit on a donkey's panniers before it tips over, or into a barge before it sinks.

If the quirky nature of one of these bookstores offers a particularly good match for your books – eg a book barge ought to be a good outlet for books about canals – exploit that natural advantage.

Nonbookstore Outlets

It's worth also considering whether your books would go down well in stores that are not bookstores at all. Many other kinds of stores choose to sell a limited range of books as part of a much more diverse product range. While this might seem a more obvious opportunity for nonfiction books (history books in relevant museums, travel books in tourist offices, etc.), it can also work well for fiction.

For example, US novelist Karen Myers' *Hounds of Annwn* fantasy series, which features a strong foxhunting theme, is stocked in equestrian and hunting equipment shops.

Similarly, historical novelist Anna Sayburn Lane has placed her debut novel, *Unlawful Things* – a thriller about the fictional quest for a lost play by Shakespeare's contemporary Christopher Marlowe - in the busy gift shop of Shakespeare's Globe Theatre in London.

Such arrangements are known in the trade as "special sales," and while these examples may seem like minor tangential diversions from the average author's marketing plan, they are potentially more powerful than they might seem. Led by executive director Brian Jud, the Association of Publishers for Special Sales (APSS) exists to help authors exploit the full power of such lateral thinking. On its website, it summarizes the publisher's (or indeed author–publisher's) dilemma as follows:

Publishers of all sizes are learning that limiting sales only to traditional channels may be the least effective and most costly way to sell books. This understanding has spawned a different way to market books, one that increases sales, revenue and profits for those who take their products to people where they buy, rather than waiting for consumers to come to them. That in essence is special-sales (non-bookstore, non-traditional) marketing.

Special-sales marketing is not a separate way of doing business. It is not even a new way of doing business. It is an integral part of overall marketing strategy, an extension of what you are probably already doing. If you are selling to bookstores now, you can sell to special markets without changing your habits or inventing new skills.

Special sales, says APSS, thus focuses not on selling through bookstores but through places "where your potential readers shop (bookstores, gift shops, catalogs), gather (seminars, libraries, associations) or work (offices, schools, hospitals)."

Exploiting special-sales opportunities to the full requires building a presence in these places in a way that will attract potential readers to buy your books. Actually making that happen can be challenging. APSS aims "to help multi-format content publishers to increase their revenue and profits through sales to non-bookstore buyers," and it has impressive success stories to share, such as that of Amy Schoen. By thinking beyond the bookstore, she found opportunities to sell her book *Get it Right This Time*, about helping single people meet their lifelong partner, to cruise ship lines, to florists, and to online dating services for use as a premium to attract new business.

APSS is a membership organization offering extensive resources and benefits in return for a modest annual fee. Find out more at its website at APSS.org. It's also an excellent source of ideas and inspiration.

Which to Choose?

Given the array of stores outlined above, which should you choose to target?

For the time-pressed indie author, focusing on large chains where book-buying is centralized might seem a more efficient use of time than schlepping round to individual indies. However, you are then pitching yourself against a much bigger field of competition, including big publishers with a proven track record in sales, a network of publishing reps visiting bookstores to pitch their catalogs, and money to spend on securing prime store space. (More about that in Chapter 6.)

You may get lucky, and you may have a standout book that will leap out from the ton of books that arrives in the buyers' offices each day. Or you may not. The most you have to lose by trying is the cost of a book and the time it takes you to prepare your covering material and submit it. But usually you'll have a better chance of gaining attention from central buyers if you've already scored some impressive successes in your home territory, both in independent bookstores and in local branches of your targeted chain.

There's a lot to be said for targeting those stores on your home territory. Being a local author adds an extra reason for them to stock your book. Local stores may be in your comfort zone, making you feel more confident, especially if they're shops that you frequent as a customer. Traveling to stores costs time and money. Target too many distant shops and your potential profit will quickly be guzzled up by your travel costs. Few of us can expect to be able to walk to many stockists, though I do know at least one author who, living in a town blessed with several bookstores, takes pleasure in cycling round them at weekends to replenish stocks.

When I say target local stores, I don't just mean local independent bookstores, because local branches of chains may also prove receptive, if you go about it in the right way with a suitable book—but more about that in Chapters 7 and 8.

But first, before we look in more detail at how to approach your chosen stores, let's consider whether and why you really want to invest the time, effort, and money into getting your books into bookstores of any kind, or whether you'd be happiest to stick with selling online—which is most indie authors' starting point—and devote time that could be spent on marketing elsewhere, marketing other formats, or writing more books.

7

HOW BOOKSTORES OPERATE
WHAT BOOKSELLERS NEED FROM PUBLISHERS

This chapter provides broad guidelines on how bookstores operate, but each country's system is a little different, so please do further research into your local territory's way of working before finalizing your decisions. The simplest way to clarify the finer details that apply to your own country is to befriend your local bookstore staff and ask them—and of course to follow appropriate publishing news sites and blogs, including ALLi's.

Wherever you are based, the best way to understand how a bookstore operates is to try to see it from the other side of the counter. Most authors have no idea what it's like unless they've served time at some point in their career as a bookseller. Those who have, such as MC Beaton and Hugh Howey, develop a lasting respect.

There's no shame in not instinctively understanding how bookstores work. How can you be expected to know unless you've had firsthand experience? The important thing is to learn about it now, so that you don't blow your chances from the outset. Once you're able to put yourself in the bookseller's shoes and see the self-published author's pitch through the bookseller's eyes, you'll not only make a more effective and efficient pitch for your book, you'll also find it easier to build a strong long-term relationship with bookstores.

A Cautionary Tale

Every bookseller in every store is likely at some point to have had a clumsy and inappropriate approach from the indie author from hell, which may have skewed their perspective of self-published books and their authors. Let's picture the scene.

On a busy, crowded Saturday, when customers are queuing at the tills, Fred Fly walks into the bookstore, straight from the door, with no real interest in any aspect of the store other than its potential to stock his book. Although he lives less than a mile away, he hasn't been in the shop since he was a schoolboy – he makes all his book purchases on Amazon - so he has to search to find the sales counter.

He joins the small queue, sighing impatiently as the lady in front of him pays for a large pile of expensive books using her well-worn store loyalty card. When he finally gains the bookseller's attention, he produces his book with a flourish, almost as if expecting a round of applause.

"I've written a book," he says, pointing proudly to his name. "That's me, Fred Fly, and I live across town from here. So I'm a local author. And I've self-published it too. So, how many copies would you like me to provide for your first order? Ten? Twenty? Fifty? I have a gross of them out in my car, so if you want to display a big pile in your window, I have plenty of stock."

The bookseller looks at the book, trying to work out what genre it's in, and what the local connection is. He also has trouble reading the title, which is in an artistic swirly print in dazzling colors. He flips it over to read the blurb, in hope of finding the missing clues. It's full of anonymous reviews—or rather, gushing quotes attributed to an anonymous "Amazon reviewer."

The bookseller's hackles rise: only this morning another potential customer, after grilling him for information about the best birdwatcher's handbook, had turned down the chance to buy the recommended book, saying "Oh, no thanks, now I know what I'm looking for, I'll order it on Amazon when I get home—it'll be much cheaper and save me carrying it."

The bookseller is conscious of the growing queue behind Fred Fly, and though he doesn't want to waste genuine customers' time, he doesn't wish to appear rude. After all, his store is renowned for its excellent customer service, a reputation he needs to maintain.

"Can you just leave your AI sheet with me please, so I can look at it later?" Fred Fly looks blank. "You know, with the salient points about the book? What's special about it? Price? Stockists? Reviews? Endorsements?"

Fred Fly frowns.

"What do you need some sheet of paper for? I'm giving you the whole book for free. Just try reading it, and I'm sure you're going to love it. All my friends do. My mother said it's the best book she's ever read."

"What about your terms? Are you offering sale or return? What discount can you offer? We expect 40% as standard."

"Forty per cent discount? After all my hard work writing it? Are you trying to be funny? No, thank you, I'll take it elsewhere, to someone who really appreciates a good book when they see it."

Exit Fred Fly, in a huff, never to darken the store's doorstep again, much to the bookseller's relief. Back at home, Fred tweets his disgust at his local bookstore's lack of support for self-published authors, tagging the store in case the bookseller sees the error of his ways and decides to order his book after all. Meanwhile the bookseller discreetly shares his experience with colleagues in a private forum, garnering sympathy and moral support and putting them on their guard for when Fred comes knocking at their bookstore door...

I'm sure no one savvy enough to read this book would ever be as crass as Fred Fly, but this fictitious case study is a fun way to illustrate the difference between the author's perspective and the bookseller's. (I should add, as in my novels, any similarity to any real person, place, or event is purely coincidental!)

It's important to note that the key deterrent here is not that the book was self-published. If a trade-published author had behaved in the same way, they would also have deserved short shrift.

An Extreme Case

Fred Fly's example is not the worst we've come across in ALLi. Just recently a bookseller's Facebook thread told of a woman who had come into his store expecting him to accept two boxes of her newly self-published autobiography for sale. She had no prior relationship with the bookstore or the bookseller, and no obvious claim to fame that might generate demand for her memoirs.

The bookseller's heart sank even further when she produced a sample book from the box: it wasn't even a book, but a spiral bound photocopy of her typescript, run off in vast quantities by the local copy shop.

"If she'd ever been inside my bookstore, or any other bookstore, and taken a look at what was on the shelves, she'd have seen for herself that this was not the sort of thing we would ever sell," said the exasperated bookseller.

Other bookseller friends were quick to condemn this as a classic case of a naive author who had not bothered to research her market or learn the rules of the game, and at the same time cursed all self-published authors by association.

Luckily for her, this particular bookseller was kindhearted and patient enough to offer sympathy and to direct her to ALLi for guidance on how to self-publish more effectively. Such incidents, as well as being personally distressing for the would-be author, are not helpful to the cause of self-publishing, because displaying the lowest common denominator tarnishes the sector as a whole.

I was quick to point out on the thread that this incident was hardly representative of the sector, and that there were plenty of self-published books produced to such professional standards that they were indistinguishable from trade-published titles. Fortunately, this particular bookseller already knew this, having had many good experiences of self-published books, and noted that his current bestseller was an indie title.

This cautionary tale may seem far-fetched, but just about every bookseller has a similar horror story to tell about an inappropriate approach with an unsaleable book. If you ever feel that a bookseller is reacting less than enthusiastically to your approach, try to view your approach through their eyes. Fred Fly may have paid a visit just before you did, putting the bookseller off self-publishing until their faith is restored by a better prospect. Make sure you are that prospect by understanding how bookstores operate so that you can get your pitch right.

To offset the balance, indie author, Di Castle, gives an example of how she approached her local bookstore the right way:

> I have always used my local bookstore, New and Secondhand Books, Station Road, Swanage, and before my book came out I visited more often and cultivated a good relationship with the owner, Jill Blanchard. I checked that the publisher had sent an advance information sheet, and said I would get the owner some Facebook likes and publicize it when she stocked my book. She has taken two deliveries direct from me of ten books and sold them, and is now on her second lot of five since Christmas. *Grandma's Poetry Book* has been in the window twice, first for a whole month before Christmas and then for a couple of weeks around Mother's Day. I take her my homespun fliers, which are targeted for her (no Amazon mention), and she has been putting them in bags when people buy other books. I abandoned Amazon for purchases and now order my books through her shop. I have promoted her on Facebook and Twitter and pop in regularly to check how many copies are there. She charges a favorable local author rate. I have my book in four other Dorset bookstores by taking in a sample copy or posting one for review preceded by a phone call. Altogether I have been delighted with how receptive these independent bookstores have been.

Scottish author Barry Hutchison has gone out of his way to create a role for his local bookstore in his business model. He said:

Although I sell most of my books online, I've commissioned my local bookstore in my nearest town of Fort William, Scotland, to handle orders for signed paperbacks - a win-win situation in which the bookstore gains extra business while saving me from a time-consuming admin task.

The Bookseller's Objectives

Whereas the author's objective is to get books stocked in a local bookstore for reasons of their own, such as validation or ambition, the bookseller's objective is far more practical: to run a successful bookstore. Your book is a tiny piece in the jigsaw of the business, and it may not even fit at all.

What makes a successful bookstore?

- attractive premises, well maintained, in a good position
- a carefully curated mix of the right books to appeal to the local clientele
- effective stock management to ensure the most profitable use of shelf space
- efficient service to customers by motivated, happy and well-informed staff with effective inter-personal skills
- strong administration and financial management skills.

What threatens a bookstore's success?

- books that won't appeal to its customer base (staff will have a very clear idea of its customers' likes and dislikes and general buying habits)
- books that don't sell but clutter up shelves that might earn more money with different stock
- books that are substandard, e.g. full of errors or which fall

apart, damaging customer goodwill and potentially driving them to shop elsewhere
- people who disrespect or waste staff time, preventing them from dealing with customers waiting to be served
- unprofitable deals, e.g. profit margins that do not cover the cost of sale.

To agree to stock a book, the bookseller must believe that it is:

- produced to professional standards, in terms of writing and production values
- a good match for the store's clientele
- offering a realistic profit margin, i.e. discount against its recommended selling price
- easy to source, ideally via the normal distributor, with new stock fast to arrive.

When you pitch your book to a bookseller, those are the considerations that will be top of their mind. Even if you are a longstanding customer, know the staff well, and buy books there all the time, if your book doesn't meet those last criteria, you're unlikely to get a good reception. If you're lucky, the bookseller will let you down gently, say encouraging things about your book, and encourage you to keep writing. If you're not so lucky, and especially if you're a stranger to the shop, you may get less sympathetic treatment, especially if there is a queue of customers behind you, waiting to pay for their purchases.

The Competition

But take heart, because trade-published books have to run the same gauntlet as you. You are all making a bid for a place on the shelf alongside other players in the industry, as if your books are participants in a vast balloon debate. It's down to you to make the case for your books not to be jettisoned.

You may think bookstores can carry a lot of stock, and a first glance at the figures suggest you're right: 20,000 in the case of a city-center store that I frequent. But think again: there are currently over 30,000,000 print book titles listed on Amazon.com. A bookstore may thus stock less than 0.1% of them—or only one in every 1,250 books that are in print.

Clearly there is only room for so many books in a bookstore, and those that are there have to pay their way. Like tenants of bookshelf space, they must sell enough copies to justify the replenishment of their stock. If a book sits on a shelf without selling any copies it's dead space, earning the bookseller a nil return, and will quickly be removed from the shelf by any bookseller wishing to stay in business. The tenant who never pays any rent should expect eviction.

Actually, it's worse than a nil return—because removing books that don't sell creates an admin load. That said, at least the bookseller doesn't have to bear the cost of the stock that hasn't sold: they purchase their stock on a sale or return basis, so that the publisher refunds them for any books that are returned unsold. This facility enables the bookseller to be ruthless about honing his stock – and it's how good bookstores thrive. (We'll discuss the sale or return policy from the indie author's perspective in Chapter 9.)

Many indies baulk at the concept of making their books available on sale or return – an option they must pick when publishing their print books via IngramSpark – but it's a historic mainstay of the book trade. Its purpose is to provide security to booksellers, encouraging them to buy in new titles and take risks on as yet unproven books – essential for publishers' business models which are based on a constant flow of new releases.

But it's not a blanket policy. Certain books, such as seasonal annuals and yearbooks, may be ordered as firm sales only, ie they are non-returnable. There are also ceilings on returns, depending on the bookstore's spend, typically 10-20%. Returned books must be in pristine condition, theoretically still saleable if sent to another store. This is because it is expensive to ship and return unsold books, and wasteful of resources, especially when many publishing houses automatically pulp all returns.

Publishers and distributors do not wish to encourage lazy buying habits. The ceiling ensures booksellers buy only what they are reasonably confident of selling. Even so, publishers encourage large orders with returns a calculated risk.

"Better terms are available to booksellers who subscribe for more copies on ordering, whether or not they sell them," says Nic Bottomley. "Therefore too many are pulped unsold. The book industry makes very efficient use of its waste, but it's still wrong to have an industry built around over-buying and pulping."

Important note: if you agree to sale or return for your books, it does not mean returned copies will be returned to you (which would at least give you some stock copies for handselling). You will effectively be charged the cost of the book, but have no book to show for it.

The size of the bookseller's workload is made even greater by the average shelf life of a book. Even those that sell well initially may grind to a halt after a few weeks, after launch publicity dies down, and are quietly dispatched when the demand slows or stops. There's usually a time constraint on returns: between three and 12 months after purchase. It's easy to think of bookshelves as static objects, but in reality they're more like revolving doors. Therefore, to stock a book for any length of time, long or short, the bookseller has to be convinced that it will earn its right to shelf space.

How Booksellers Buy Books

So the obvious next question is: how do booksellers choose their stock? Like any other retailer, they carefully choose and curate their product range to best please their target customers. No one knows a store's customers as well as the booksellers who work there, and each store will hold different stock. Even in a chain, where book-buying is done centrally, the buyers will take into consideration the target audience of each store and stock it accordingly, rather than sending out the same stock to every branch. Centralized chains may or may not give a certain degree of autonomy to local managers, on the basis of their local knowledge.

Where are booksellers **most** likely to find out about new books?

- trade publications (*Publishers Weekly* in the US, *The Bookseller* in the UK)
- national press (*The New York Times, US Today, The Times, The Guardian*, etc)
- regional and local press
- social media
- bookseller friends and colleagues (most booksellers will have many friends in the trade)
- publishers (via websites, catalogs and visiting sales reps).

All of these will carry a certain amount of authority, a kind of third-party approval that will help build the bookseller's confidence that a certain book is a safe bet to stock. The publisher is the only one who makes a human pitch to the bookseller, in the form of sales representatives who contact or visit booksellers directly to promote their latest batch of books. These reps are largely professional, knowledgeable, slick—and respectful of the bookseller's workload.

They also take the trouble to get to know each shop and its customer base, so that they can pitch the most appropriate books.

"I just had a rep in here who pitched me for his publisher's top 100 titles of this season with just 10 seconds per book," Hereward Corbett told me, appreciative of the efficient use of his time.

Nic Bottomley estimates that in the UK, publishers' catalogs offer 4,500 new titles each month, with 1,200 of those personally pitched by visiting reps with one sentence per book.

It is possible to buy the services of an independent rep for your self-published book, but you'll have to sell a lot of books to justify the cost. If buying distribution services, you need to note that there are two kinds on offer:

1. full-service distribution, in which a rep makes in-store visits and actually sells your books to booksellers
2. wholesale distribution, which makes your books available through the distributor's catalog, but doesn't includes the services of a rep to sell them.

To be clear, KDP Print, IngramSpark and Lightning Source offer wholesale distribution as standard, i.e. your books will be listed passively in their database. Further services such as promotional catalog entries are available as an extra chargeable option.

As an aside, when you are uploading your print book to IngramSpark, bear in mind that it will take longer for your new book to appear in the buying databases used by booksellers than it will for your book to go live on the Amazon storefront. This is because the data has a longer and more complex journey: it's not just a question of populating IngramSpark's database, but it trickling out through distributors and wholesalers' records. IngramSpark sends out new data once a week, but that's just the start of the process. Therefore upload your print book as soon as you can, at least two or three weeks before your on-sale date. That way the metadata will still go out and preorders can be collected, and your book will go live at the same time as its Amazon equivalent, rather than lagging a few weeks behind. This will demonstrate to booksellers that you are not giving priority to Amazon but are paying due consideration to bricks-and-mortar stores.

"Full-service distribution is what most indies want but can't afford," says Robin Cutler, Director of IngramSpark. "You need a certain level of sales to support it and to be successful already. There's a reason for traditional publishers to be so slow and long term with publishing and promoting books: to justify full-service sales."

Full-Service Distribution

IngramSpark recommends that you need to have run up sales of about 50,000 books as the entry level to justify the cost of full-service distribution and be prepared to offer sale or return.

It's also worth noting that books actively "pushed" in this way, rather than ordered spontaneously by the bookstore, are more likely to be returned unsold. An average 60% return rate. Gulp!

To have your books featured alongside trade-published books, sold by a dedicated and specialist in-house team directly into bookstores of all kinds, sounds extremely attractive, but the economics of print-on-demand publishing probably won't allow for full-service distribution unless your book is in a high-pricing genre, you are established as a consistent bestseller, or ideally both.

Even if you are confident of attracting sufficient sales, you'll need to be prepared to fit in with the conventional timing of the way trade-published books are sold to bookstores, i.e. up to six months in advance of a book's publication date. There may be other criteria to meet, such as being required to supply a large number of printed copies up front, so there is ready-made stock to sell, thus guaranteeing promised delivery times to buyers, which might not be possible via print-on-demand.

To use either of these services, your books must be published via Ingram or Matador respectively.

Be sure to read all of the details before making a commitment—and be wary of any company offering full-service distribution at a surprisingly low cost. Lesser companies have been known to sell the service without following it through, simply warehousing your stock instead of actively selling it to bookstores.

In such a competitive industry, where so many publishers compete for shelf space for their protégés, it's also in publishers' interests to build good long-term relationships with booksellers, in hope of always getting a good reception for their brand. The same bookseller I mentioned before made me smile when he told me his response to an unsolicited phone call from a publisher's rep:

"What can we do to help your bookstore sell more books?" asked the rep.

"Get rid of me, for a start," quipped the self-deprecating bookseller.

Although booksellers will be targeted directly by the agents of publishers, they generally don't order books from the publisher, but through a preferred distributor or wholesaler. This simplifies paperwork—a single invoice and a single delivery for a whole raft of books from multiple publishers. It also makes life simpler for the publishers, because the costs of consolidated shipments can be shared.

Conspicuous by its absence from the list above is the author. That's because booksellers don't usually deal—or want to deal—with authors individually, unless those authors have been invited to do a book-signing or other event in-store, or unless the author has developed a good personal relationship with a store. We indie authors may believe that no one is as powerful an advocate as we are for our books, but sending individual authors to pitch for their books to individual bookstores, with one-off invoices and deliveries, is really anathema to a system built around consolidation, to the benefit of all parties.

Historically, indie authors and booksellers have struggled to efficiently print, stock and provide readers with titles they want, when they want it and at a great price. However, today's technology can open new ways to streamline book distribution, creating cost-savings and efficiencies.

Recognising that the narrow profit margins on POD print make it difficult for indies to offer a high discount, IngramSpark can offer volume discounts for indie authors to enable them to keep all their print needs in one place, rather than seeking other printers for personal orders for handselling at events.

IngramSpark also provides an alternative system for bookstores that would like to order POD books at a greater profit: the IngramContent.com/ipage distribution system. ipage is an easy-to-use online search, order and account management platform which not only means more choice for independent bookstores but also, in most cases, better terms—including free shipping on any order size.

According to Ingram Content's Marketing Manager, Andy Bromley, ipage enables indie authors and booksellers to work more easily in a mutually beneficial partnership that is more financially worthwhile for both, by cutting out the middleman for Ingram publishing POD books.

Originally available in the US, ipage is now spreading further afield, most recently to the UK, giving UK retailers the ability to order in GBP straight from Ingram's catalog of 14 million titles. Booksellers are still using their old systems—going through Gardners and other wholesalers—but Ingram hopes to win more of them over, which would give indie authors better visibility in bookstores across the UK.

"Using Ingram for POD and ordering systems like ipage helps indie authors to get their books out there, while keeping costs down, Bromley says. "Bookstores know that a POD paperback book can be printed and shipped from our facilities, usually within 48 hours, and is never out of stock."

While ipage is a useful option, it does not suit everybody, not least because it is still available only in a handful of territories around the world.

"Most retailers do not want to register yet another account, and thus want to go through one of the established distributors," reports Ritesh Kala, an indie author and publisher in India. "It makes it that much easier to get the books stocked if you are with the local distributors." For now, anyway. Though Ingram plans to change that.

Special Orders

When we visit a bookshop and peruse its shelves, it's easy to assume that customers buy only what's displayed on the shelves – ie those books routinely ordered into stock and replaced as they sell.

Not so. Look behind the trade counter and you will see shelves full of special orders: books ordered in at the request of individual customers – books that would otherwise not be in stock. Regular customers in particular will readily ask the bookseller to order in a title that is out of stock, or which has not yet been stocked – books they may have come in expressly to buy.

Provided the profit margin justifies the effort (which it usually will), any bookseller are happy to help, as a special order means a guaranteed, risk-free sale. You may be surprised to learn the typical percentage of a bookstore's sales comprised of special orders: one bookseller I polled cited 40% of his store's sales. A more typical proportion is between 15% and 20% for a town centre store with a regular and loyal clientele, and perhaps 5% for those in malls.

"It depends on a store's clientele," says Hereward Corbett of the Yellow-Lighted Bookshop in Tetbury, UK, " whether it's more review-led or backlist-driven."

This is good news for indies: if you are unable to get your books stocked permanently, you can still get them into the hands of readers through bookstores' special orders. And better still: as it's a firm sale, it's not crucial to offer sale or return. You might even get away with a lower discount – but we'll talk more about financial considerations in a later chapter.

Your Book in Bookstores

Whether or not you promote your self-published books to booksellers via the services of a rep, and whether your books are stocked year-round or bought in only on special order, it is essential to your success that your book looks fit to display in a bookstore, and the next chapter will help you ensure that your books truly are bookstore ready.

8

MAKE YOUR BOOK BOOKSTORE READY

MEETING THE BOOKSELLER'S NEEDS

A devout man who has fallen on hard times prays to his god. "Please, God, I've been a faithful servant. I've been good to my family, worked hard in my job, and helped my neighbor and my community. Would it be so hard for you to make it possible for me to win the lottery?" God's reply: "My son, if you want to win the lottery, it helps if you buy a ticket."

Is your book bookstore ready? It may seem to be stating the obvious, but a surprising number of self-published books fall at the first hurdle by simply not being up to the professional standards demanded by bookstores. Most booksellers have been approached by hopeful indie authors clutching books that have been far from market ready. Sometimes they don't even have a physical book to show the bookseller, unlike the trade publisher's rep, who will have ARCs (advance review copies) issued pre-publication to entice the support of stockists and reviewers. To expect them to take on a self-published book is challenging enough, but to get them to commit to a book they've never seen is beyond optimistic.

Booksellers also complain of being shown books that simply are not fit to be seen in a bookstore, whether because the cover is unprofessional or inappropriate for the genre, the layout inside is unprofessional, or the price is not viable in a bookstore setting. No matter how wonderful the content is (an obvious point to add to your checklist!), if it's not presented right—and by right I mean in a way that will make readers buy it—the bookseller won't be interested. Such behavior also puts the bookseller in a very difficult position and creates barriers for your future relationship.

So help yourself. When your book is up against stiff competition from millions of others for a space on any bookstore shelf, it makes sense to ensure your book is bookstore ready before casting it into the ring.

That means it should pass muster as if it were a professionally trade-published book. Yes, we know that self-published books can and should be as good as trade-published ones, pushing the boundaries of convention and commercialism, refusing to be constrained by genre, and so on—but that doesn't mean we may flout any of the professional standards that big publishers set, in terms not only of the writing, but also the many other elements that are the responsibility of the self-publishing author: editing, proofreading, formatting, cover design, title, and blurb. The rest of this chapter suggests a series of questions to ask yourself and will help you ensure your books provide the right answers.

Does Your Book Pass the Identity Parade Test?

This test may seem anathema to staunch indie authors, fiercely protective and proud of their indie status, but I strongly advise you to submit to it. If you put your book on a display table in a bookstore among those published by big publishing companies, would it blend in? Would it fit on the shelves, the same size as other books in its genre? Would it recognizably belong in an obvious niche? If it's a fluffy romance, is it in light and airy colors? If it's horror, is its cover suitably ominous?

Are you sure you're aiming at the right niche for the content of your book? Or even more than one niche?

If your book falls outside of any standard genre, booksellers, like publishers, won't know what to do with it or where to display it to ensure interested readers might find it. This doesn't mean that you need to blindly follow what everyone else is doing. After all, you are an indie, and the freedom to play things how you wish is one of the great joys of your status. But if you're going to be wildly different, expect a harder sell to the bookseller, and don't be surprised if your book is rejected as unshelvable. It's your prerogative to be as different as you like, but just be aware of the implications.

Novelist Rohan Quine has executed a remarkable coup in having his cross-genre novels stocked in a flagship store, by convincing them that it was appropriate in fantasy/sci-fi, literary fiction, and horror. They even went the extra mile by displaying his title *The Platinum Raven* alongside Edgar Allan Poe's novel *The Raven* – and a large stuffed raven!

If your book is very different from trade publishing norms, perhaps that's a sign that bookstore distribution is not for you. Author and poet Dan Holloway, whose more conventional thriller had been given prominent displays in his local chain, did not expect to get the same treatment for *Evie and Guy*, his experimental novel written entirely in numbers. Not getting stocked in a bookstore was not going to deflect him from his creative intentions.

Of course, there's always the exception to the rule, with the book that is so radically different that, while there is no obvious place for a bookstore to display it, it leaps off the shelves and becomes a groundbreaking bestseller, the leader of the pack. Surely there was once the first adult coloring book that furrowed the brows of booksellers everywhere, before those brave enough to stock it found it quickly boosted their profits. Early adopters were ahead of the pack in setting aside not just shelf space but whole areas of their stores to showcase the fast-growing range.

Another genre-busting curiosity comes along every so often to take up the mantle of the maverick that made good. But the vast majority of books sold in bookstores will look like, well, books sold in bookstores.

Have You Avoided Rookie Errors

You may write, design, and present your book to match the norms in your target genre, but does it meet professional standards? Or would it jump out from the crowd shouting "Self-published! Home-made! Cover flung together on Word!" You know the answer I'm looking for...

Cover design needs to be distinctive not only from the front, but when looking at the spine too. When we're selling our books online, we're used to regarding the thumbnail of the front cover as the critical factor, because on online book retail sites, books are effectively all displayed with the cover facing the reader. In bookstores, however, the vast majority are spine out. Too many indies neglect the spine. An alarming number have no spine copy or images at all, even when the spine width is plenty wide enough to take it. In POD books, the spine needs to be a greater width than in litho printing to accommodate copy and graphics to allow for greater variance of movement during the production process.

"Ensure the spine's design echoes the book's cover format – font, colour, significant graphics," advises recently retired bookseller Peter Snell. "Also make sure your book is a standard size so that it fits on a bookstore's shelves."

Bookseller Hereward Corbett tries to let down gently any indies who don't make the grade: "I often point out to visiting indies what strong competition they are up against. Trade publishers spend hundreds of thousands on cover design, for example. If you can't match that quality, perhaps a bookstore isn't the best starting point for you to try to sell your books."

Too many books give away their origins by making simple mistakes that would never appear in a trade-published book. Comic Sans for a historical novel? It's been known to happen. Prefacing the author's name with "Mr/Mrs/Ms"? That's only appropriate if it's part of your pen-name, eg novelist Miss Read), or by using inappropriate fonts on the cover for the type of book. Also putting "by" before the author's name is unconventional, unless you are also naming the illustrator on the cover, so that it becomes clear which party is responsible for which aspect of the book. This often applies to children's picture books or highly illustrated books for adults.

Other rookie errors include forewords or acknowledgments sections that read like a bad Oscar acceptance speech. Keep those short and functional. Do not thank everyone you know, or mention what a trial and a triumph it has been to write your first book, or the fact that you've published it yourself because no one else would. Do not add a PS asking readers to email you when they find errors. There shouldn't be any. You may think all those things, but if you need to say them, put them elsewhere, such as in reader newsletters, where your target booksellers won't see. Ask yourself: what would [insert name of your most idolized author here] do?

Fortunately, such basic mistakes happen less often these days. We're by no means taking all the credit for this, but since ALLi was founded in 2012 with a mission of excellence and ethics in self-publishing, the standards of author-published books has risen. Indie authors today are better informed, more sophisticated and more experienced, and though there are plenty of rank amateurs around, they drop out of the game when they understand the level of work involved.

But there will always be a large number of indie authors who don't know or don't care about publishing craft and thus a great number of books that look and feel self-published. These tarnish the rest by association. Make sure yours does not fall into that category.

Does It Match the Needs of the Store?

Assuming that your book looks a perfect fit for a standard bookstore genre, and is written and produced to professional standards, you still need to ask yourself whether it's a good match for the bookstores you wish to target. Booksellers curate their stock to suit their local market, and they know their clientele better than you ever will. A book that is a perfect fit at one branch on the east coast of the States, for example, may be a nonstarter on the west coast. This is particularly true for small independent stores, where purchasing decisions are made at local level, rather than by a remote head office. (By the way, do not discount the wisdom of the head office on account of its geographical distance—its buyers have at their disposal vast amounts of very accurate data about local purchasing patterns, gathered via loyalty cards and research both within their stores and elsewhere.)

In most cases, we'd recommend that the first bookstores you target should be those on your home turf, where you should ideally already be a familiar face and a known customer. (If not, it's time you started shopping local.) That way you can build your confidence and experience before taking your book further afield.

Should you wish to dive into chain bookstores with centralized purchasing, you will be unlikely to be able to make that pitch in person. Instead, you'll need to target the appropriate person by email and post. If so, do your research first to obtain the right name for the buyer of books in your genre. In large genres, there may be more than one. Bear in mind that the competition for attention of central purchasers will be much greater than at a local store, so your pitch will need to be even more carefully prepared. Phone the head office and grill the receptionist to get the name of the most appropriate person.

Even where there is centralized buying, if you are able to chat up a local member of staff, you may gain an introduction to the appropriate central buyer, and even a recommendation. Branch staff also talk to each other, so if your book does well in one branch, you may find orders coming in from other stores following their recommendations.

Even where chains practice centralized buying as a matter of policy, there is likely to be a member of staff in every branch with responsibility for local buying. Speaking at the 2019 Futurebook conference in London, James Daunt confirmed that every Waterstones store has a member of staff who can make buying decisions. Even when targeting chains, clarify whether you may approach resident buyers in local branches. Success with one store's buyer can lead to uptake in other branches, as staff share success stories and personal favourites with their colleagues elsewhere in the chain.

Do You Have a Plausible Publisher's Imprint—and Do You Need One?

One of the questions often discussed among indie authors seeking bookstore listings is whether you should publish your book under an imprint—that is a publishing company's name—rather than your own. One school of thought says that presenting your book this way adds weight by looking more professional and conventional. The other argument protests that you should wear your book's self-published status with pride, declaring yourself to be proudly author and publisher, unadorned.

As with so much in the indie publishing sector, the decision is entirely up to you—whatever you feel comfortable with. You must, of course, comply with any local trading and taxation regulations in your own country. In some regions, it's simple and straightforward to assume a trading name, while actually trading as an individual; in others it's more complex.

I've taken the imprint route myself, naming my Hawkesbury Press after my home village, which is appropriate for my cosy village mystery novels. It has its own website where I've made clear the nature of the organisation, so there can be no confusion or accusations of deceit. Even so, I've been bemused and gratified by the perceptions of strangers. When a customer services assistant in a store asked me my plans for the evening, I told him I was off to a writers' group meeting. "What do you write?" he asked. I pulled a copy of my first in series from my bag to show him. When he flipped it over to read the blurb, he noticed the imprint. "Ah, Hawkesbury Press. Yes, they do good books, don't they?" What could I do but agree?

If you do decide to take the imprint route, make sure before choosing your imprint that it's not already taken by someone else, that it sounds like a proper and professional company, and that it's appropriate to the books you'll be publishing. Naming your imprint Fluffy after your cat will detract from the impact of horror titles. Think long term when picking your name—if you're likely to publish across a wide range of genres, don't restrict yourself by choosing a single-genre name. Vampire Press may be fine for your fantasy thrillers, but won't look so great should you diversity into cookery books.

Do You Have Your Own ISBNs?

Related to the question of imprints is the issue of ISBNs. What are ISBNs? ISBNs are internationally recognized book identifiers, each unique to a particular book. One part of the ISBN identifies the registered publisher of the book, while another indicates the specific book. ISBNs are issued by a single supplier in each country, for a set price. In some countries they are issued free of charge. When you order your supply of ISBNs, you specify the name of the publisher at the point of ordering. ISBNs are not transferable.

There is only one ISBN supplier per country, and you must buy your ISBNs from your country of residence at whatever rate they dictate. Lucky you if your national government subsidizes ISBN costs, as some do to encourage cultural development, or even issues them free.

The value of an ISBN becomes clear when you realize that it is the key that unlocks all the information a bookstore will require about any book. If a customer can provide your ISBN, the bookseller will be able to identify your book, even if the customer can't remember the correct title, spell the author name, or describe what the cover looks like.

This is great stuff, of course. But there are occasions when it can work against you. For example, if you have published your print book solely via Amazon's KDP Print, using the ISBN supplied free of charge, when booksellers look up your book's ISBN they will instantly see Amazon listed as your publisher.

This immediately creates barriers to buying. Many booksellers will, as a matter of principle, refuse to stock books bearing the KDP Print imprint because they perceive Amazon to be a rival and a threat to their business.

Secondly, even if they are not averse to stocking it on principle, they will be unable to order it via their usual distributors. Yes, anyone may order it from Amazon's website, but that would be at the retail price, bypassing any chance of a profit margin.

Many newcomers to self-publishing see the ISBN as an avoidable cost, not realizing the implications for bookstores, but ALLi strongly recommends you buy your own, so that you or your chosen imprint is registered as the publisher of record.

Using Amazon KDP and IngramSpark Together

ALLi recommends that you produce your POD print books simultaneously through IngramSpark and KDPP, using the same ISBN for both, the one you bought and registered under your own author name or publishing imprint. That way, when a bookseller searches for your ISBN, you (not Amazon) will show up as the publisher of record.

This is important as many bookstores don't like to stock Amazon books. You also avoid your book being listed as out of stock or "currently unavailable" on Amazon. This message usually suggests it may be weeks before your book is available, or even that it is unknown when, or whether, it will be back in stock. This deters orders from customers used to prompt delivery.

Yes, this is unhelpful to authors who use IngramSpark for distribution, and it's a sobering reminder that Amazon's priority is to provide a satisfactory experience for customers (readers) and bring as many authors as possible to its own systems, rather than to help authors reach readers or readers find books through pathways that are more profitable for others.

When you set your print book up in both services, bear in mind that it will inevitably take longer for the metadata and files to permeate the distributors', wholesalers' and retailers' databases fed by IngramSpark than the Amazon databases fed by KDP Print. This is because KDP is owned by Amazon so it's effectively an in-house transfer of data, whereas IngramSpark has no control over all those third parties' systems.

IngramSpark sends out its latest data files once a week (this has just changed from once at the start of each month), so if you want the two versions of your book to appear simultaneously on the sites fed by IS and on Amazon's storefronts, set your IS data up sufficiently in advance to allow for the longer process. You can synchronise when your book goes on sale in all those outlets by setting the same on-sale date on IS and KDP. "Letting the metadata flow out before the sales date is the best practice," advises Andy Bromley.

There is more advice on this topic in ALLi's guide to *Choose A Self-Publishing Service*, downloadable for free by members in the member zone or on sale in other editions and to non-members in the Self-Publishing Advice Centre Bookshop: SelfPublishingAdvice.org/shop. There are several detailed blog posts in the ALLi Author Advice Centre that give more details on this important subject. Just type "KDP Print Ingram" in the SelfPublishingAdvice.org blog search box to keep up with the latest updates.

Once you've published your books using your own ISBNs, there's a second (optional) stage to attend to: adding a summary description of the book to the central ISBN records held by the company through which you acquired your ISBNs. Obviously you will have already input information about your books elsewhere online, including the dashboards of your chosen production platforms, and this data is passed on by those platforms to distributors and wholesalers from whose databases booksellers place their orders.

However, beware that if you do this, it will override any data sent by your distribution platform, so it may be counterproductive and not the best use of your time.

Have You Priced Your Books Right?

No matter how perfect your print book looks, if its price is inappropriate, bookstores will shy away from stocking it. Too expensive compared with similar books in its genre and it won't look competitive; too cheap and there'll be no room for a decent margin for the bookstore (or for you). Pricing print books is harder than pricing ebooks because they cost more to supply, for obvious reasons: materials and production cost much more than a digital file, and they also cost more to transport. The larger your book, the more challenging it will be to make it profitable, especially in POD runs, where the unit cost is generally higher than in traditional print runs. If printing any part of the interior in color, your choice of standard or premium color production needs to be carefully considered to keep the sales price viable.

Fortunately, distributors like Lightning Source, IngramSpark and KDP Print make the task easier by providing a ready reckoner to help you adjust your price and tweak your discounts to suit your financial requirements, and so provide a safety net against loss. It's also prudent not to print your retail price on your cover, in case you decide to raise or lower it at a later date. Bookstores will be able to gather your price when they scan the barcode on your book, and they'll most likely hand price it with a label-printing gun so that their customers know the price before they buy.

When you set your discounts with the distributors, you get to choose from a preset range. Usually 30% is the minimum, but most bookstores expect at least 40%, and the top rate is an eye-watering 55%.

Bear in mind that these rates don't mean the remaining 70%/60%/45% is all yours. Your publishing platform will charge you the production cost, of course, so your own margin will actually be much lower. Take heart, though, that it's still likely to be far more than the 5% of cover price that you'd typically earn from a publishing contract with one of the Big Five.

Also note that the discount is what is offered to the distributor or wholesaler, not the bookstore. The wholesaler will take its service fee out of that discount, and the remainder of the discount is what goes to the bookstore. The more players there are in the distribution chain, the less the bookstore will get—although the total discount will always be what you determined in the first place. You may be reassured to know that you will be paid when the wholesaler pays, and not when the book is eventually bought by the end user—the bookstore customer.

Whatever discount you set on your IngramSpark dashboard, you have no way of knowing exactly what percentage ends up in the bookseller's till, because that will depend on (a) how many middlemen there are between IS and the bookseller (just a distributor or a wholesaler too) (b) what terms the bookseller has agreed with their supplier – some booksellers prefer a lower discount and a higher number of allowable returns, or a higher discount with fewer returns.

IngramSpark doesn't know that either – it's a private arrangement between those parties further down the distribution chain.

If you're wondering why IS doesn't supply directly to booksellers, and so cut out any middlemen (and their share of the takings), it's because most booksellers prefer to buy from wholesalers rather than direct from publishers. Although IngramSpark is a global company, there are different wholesalers in the various territories they serve. That is why when setting up your print books on their dashboard, you should price them in all the currencies listed.

Remember, IS, unlike Amazon, is not a retailer – it is a printer that has no direct relationship with the end-user in the process: the reader. Nor does IS deal in any products other than books – another key difference between their two business models.

Try not to get too hung up about discounts and returns, but keep an eye on the trading data on your IS account, and feel free to change the rates you set if you think it would help your sales.

IngramSpark's Andy Bromley sets the matter in perspective:

> Going over 50% wholesale discount is optimal for book sales and therefore that advice is correct from a certain perspective. However, it might not be right for you and depends on a range of things. Writing a good book and marketing it well is far more important than offering 55% vs 40%. I would advise authors not to go too low because that can cause issues but equally don't feel you need to max out on the discount, only to make little return. Experiment and share what you feel works for you.

And one final note about comparative pricing for your KDP and IS paperbacks: you are not obliged to price-match the two, although if you offer your print copy at a lower price via IS than via KDP, Amazon reserve the right to price-match. That said, you'd be unlikely to want to undercut your KDP price via IS, because you have to accommodate a trade discount.

Can You Prove You'll Be Driving Customers In?

Bestselling American thriller writer Diane Capri is sanguine about the issue of getting books into bookstores: "To me, the big issue is not so much getting the books onto shelves, but getting them from the shelf into the buyer's shopping bag and out the door. That's where the real challenge lies. If we could come up with a workable answer to that one, my guess is the booksellers would be glad to stock the books."

Therefore, use every resource that you can to demonstrate to your target bookstore that your book will be in demand. Share great reviews, press cuttings, news of public events, past and present. One neat and accessible way to do this is via the advance information (AI) sheet, a regular tool of the trade for publishers' reps, providing an at-a-glance summary of the key selling points of a book in a single A4 sheet.

Do You Have Compelling AI Sheets?

It's standard practice in the publishing trade to produce what's usually referred to as an AI in the run-up to a new book's launch, either on its own, or with a free ARC of the book. Whether or not you choose to offer a free sample of the book (and you should do that only if you're sure one is wanted, so as to avoid waste), it's definitely worth producing an AI sheet for a self-published book.

They're just as useful for indie authors as for big publishers. Why should we operate any differently, when there is this tried-and-trusted formula for effective communication with reviewers and booksellers?

The AI sheet is a single sheet of A4 paper, printed one-sided, ideally in color, but sometimes mono for the sake of economy. The AI sheet has three main uses:

1. to entice early reviewers to agree to read and review a book (the actual book may then be sent only to those who agree in advance to review it)
2. to accompany ARCs, making it super-easy for reviewers to include the correct information in any reviews they write up

3. to encourage and enable booksellers to place orders easily by providing a persuasive sales pitch coupled with practical details of how to order.

As well as being distributed to reviewers and booksellers, AI sheets may also be made available as downloads from the press and publicity sections of publishers' websites. This enables any potential reviewer or stockist to print off one for their own use at any time. As an indie, make sure you put yours on your website too.

The typical AI sheet includes a cover image, title, and author name, plus a brief overview of a book, an author bio, some testimonials, and technical data (ISBN, price, launch date, formats, etc.), plus contact details in case of query. You may also include an author photo as an optional extra. Not all publishers do, but for the indie author, I think adding a photo is a great idea, as it's more likely to be you taking your book into the store. It's also a great way of helping booksellers remember you and put the right face to the right name, further down the line.

Try to echo the style and font of your book on its AI sheet, at least for headlines and images, so that the two are a recognizable pair. Keep the body copy in a common serif font, though, such as Times New Roman or Garamond, to make the information easy to read once it's caught the reviewer or bookseller's eye.

All this information is presented in an orderly, logical manner to provide an at-a-glance summary of the features and benefits of a new book, in an attractive yet familiar and digestible form that busy reviewers and booksellers can absorb quickly and accurately.

Offering an AI sheet also adds professional credibility to self-published books and small indie press imprints. Providing one to a prospective bookseller or reviewer is a clear indication that we understand how they operate and that we will be easy to work with. It shows we speak the bookseller's language. It shows we respect reviewers' time and needs.

Unlike so many other marketing materials, AI sheets cost next to nothing to produce and distribute. You can knock one up on your own computer, print it off on your home or office printer, and add it to your own author website, or, if you publish under an imprint, on that imprint's website—or both. If you have a page for each of your books on your author website, it's a matter of moments to add a download of the AI sheet as a clickable option.

Can You Maintain Momentum?

While the AI sheet may help you get your book stocked, you need to do all you can to get it to shift off the shelves once it's there, to encourage a repeat buying pattern.

Make sure you tell local people where your book is to be found. List stockists on your website. When a new bookstore starts stocking your title, announce the fact on social media and tag the bookstore. Include stockists' details on leaflets and other promotional material, as appropriate. Offer events to your stockists. Think about ways you can collaborate with your stockists to generate sales.

Less effective tactics, such as authors surreptitiously rearranging shelves where their books are stocked, are common. In *The Bookshop Book*, Jen Campbell quotes Ian Rankin saying, "You can always tell when you're traveling which authors have been through the airport bookstores before you, because their books are the ones facing out on all the shelves."

Even cheekier, and hardly effective, are those authors who secretly plant their own books in stores while no one's looking, in the hope that someone will want to buy it, take it to the till, where the bookseller will fail to find it on their stock list, wonder why, when it's clearly in demand, and formally place an order for more.

If cheeky is your tune, don't overstep the mark and alienate customers or booksellers. Too many indie authors trying too hard, or disrespecting people's time and attention, is one of the reasons that many bookstores now treat self-published authors with caution.

This applies to fellow and sister authors too, as thriller writer Alison Morton reports:

I've been door-stepped in bookstores by inexpert indies. One even followed me round my local chain store, demanding I should buy his book "in solidarity." Bleating and whinging doesn't work.

Take the time to think out a strategy that will work and implement it.

Is It Easy to Buy in and Maintain Stock?

So now all the bookseller has to do is keep buying in more books—easy, right? Or is it?

To make sure that it's feasible and practical for the bookseller to maintain stocks of your book, the simplest solution is to make it available to order via the bookseller's usual distributor, so that buying your book will just be one extra line on the regular bulk order and invoice, rather than requiring a separate invoice just for your book. As I mentioned earlier, raising paperwork, dealing with invoices, and paying bills all costs the bookseller time and money.

It may be a helpful analogy to compare this task with your own buying practices, such as your weekly grocery shop. In the twenty-first century, most people buy the majority of their groceries from one store, and pay for it all at the till with a single card payment. Yes, we complain about waiting at the checkout, but think how much harder it would be if, for every item, you had to pay at a separate till, in a separate transaction. Or, if certain items were never available from the supermarket, but had to be obtained from a separate small shop round the corner. It wouldn't take much to persuade you, time-pressed as you are, to forget the smaller shops and just field a substitute that was available in the supermarket.

Yes, there are plenty of shoppers who still favor small indie shops and farmers' markets, but that's not the point. If you want to maximize your sales in bookstores, you need to make life easy for the way booksellers buy in.

Making your books available via their usual distributor assures booksellers that new stock will arrive quickly, so that they don't have to keep any customers waiting. It also looks professional—as if you're a part of the core trade, rather than a market stallholder standing hopefully on the periphery of the supermarket car park.

Next question: how do you make your book available via the distributor? There are two ways. The hard way is to become a regular supplier to the distributor and manage stock yourself. NB this requires you to be able to dispatch just-in-time deliveries all year round. The easy option is to publish your book through a distribution platform that deals directly with the wholesalers for you. The most significant of these are Lightning Source and IngramSpark, the latter a subsidiary of the former. Lightning Source is designed to service small to large publishing companies, and IngramSpark is more geared up to the single indie author or very small publishing firm. These services also allow you to specify your discount rates for each geographical territory, so that bookstores will know without having to ask you whether your rates suit them.

However, it does give you wider choice in terms of the production of your books by freeing you of the restrictions imposed by POD facilities. While POD is adequate for most self-publishers' purposes, if you particularly want to supply a higher quality product, eg using thicker stock, different cover materials, special cover effects such as embossing or spot laminating, or a non-standard trim size, a litho print book specialist is the answer.

A litho printer is also likely to yield a lower unit price than POD once you get over a certain quantity, as it offers greater economies of scale. But the disadvantage is that you will need to order high volume – think hundreds or thousands.

A striking contrast with a POD printer like IngramSpark, whose average print run is 1.7 books.

British novelist Jane Davis also took this route for her literary fiction novels to achieve higher production qualities and greater control than POD allowed. She printed 200 of each of her titles. As part of its service to her, Clays registered all the titles in distributor Gardners' catalog, and all orders are then fulfilled from Gardners' stock system. (Search the ALLi blog for Jane's detailed analysis of the process including costs and benefits. As an aside, Clays also offer POD as well as consignment printing.)

POD printing is usually more economical up to about 500 copies. Over 500 – certainly over 1,000 – consignment printing usually makes more sense. When weighing up, bear in mind that print cost is not the only consideration. There are other costs. "A traditional distributor will take anything from 15% to 25% of net sales for the right to use their distribution services," says Andy Bromley. "If you know you can sell 10K+ copies per year, traditional distribution is more economical. But that's less than 0.1% of books published."

If investing in consignment print runs, the clear message is: choose your quantity carefully to avoid being overwhelmed with unsold stock.

Orna Ross, who used Clays to produce a special gift edition of her novel *The Secret Rose*, cautions: "It's crucial to have your distribution outlets sorted before investing in short order print – and to do your sums. Although I was delighted with my experiment producing a premium gift book, it only worked financially for me because much of the cost was crowdfunded up front. Shifting enough copies to make a decent profit in print is still challenging for indie authors, whether it's POD or consignment print."

Some authors prefer the potential for greater profit over the convenience of POD and remote fulfilment. Scottish author Margaret Skea shares her perspective:

Doing my own print run and having the books warehoused by a distributor which connects to Gardners isn't either costly or time-consuming. (Gardners keep a small stock themselves which means they are always available on Amazon directly as opposed to third-party sellers.) I don't spend any time on the Gardners angle, nor do I have a direct account with them. The unit cost per book is much lower than POD, by over £3 per book, and the quality is excellent, the books are readily available to any bookshop in the UK and the distribution charge I pay to the distributor is much less than if I had to post a book myself. They take 15% of the net price of a book. So for a book that retails at £10, the store will pay the distributor £6 and I will get about £5. The print cost of the latest book (464 pages) is about £2.60, so my profit is £2.40. If I sell the same book direct, at events, etc, I get a whopping £7.40.

In contrast POD at that length of book comes in at almost £6 including postage. So for events, etc, if I did POD my profit would only be £4 and it wouldn't really be worth having them in bookshops at all. The distributor covers the cost of getting the book to the shop.

If I want a box of books sent to a festival or whatever and I'm going to be paid directly for them, I ask for them to be sent at no charge, and the courier cost works out at about 50p per book. For me, it's win-win. I don't have a garage full of books either. (The print runs I generally do are 500.)

For a book sent to Amazon by Gardners, I get the same royalty/profit as I do from any other shop, but for a POD book sold by Amazon, my royalty is only £1.29.

Assuming you answer "yes" to all the questions posed in this chapter, let's consider how to make that all-important pitch to your chosen bookstore with a handy checklist in Chapter 8.

9

HOW TO PITCH YOUR BOOK
PREPARATION & PERSUASION

Drawing on all that you've read here so far, you now need to summon up all your courage, optimism, and determination and go for it. Here's a step-by-step guide to help you walk through the process like you've been doing it all your life…

Assemble Your Ammunition

It's show and tell time! Along with a pristine copy of your book, pack up your AI sheet to provide an at-a-glance summary of all the key data about your book, plus any marketing collateral: local media coverage, early reviews, and endorsements from respected authors in your field… Anything that will serve as objective proof of its worth as a saleable, profit-making resource in any bookstore.

Prepare Your Questions in Advance

Think of all the questions a bookstore buyer might ask you, and have your Q&A ready prepared in your head. Why should the store stock your book? Where should your book sit on the shelves—which genre?

Is there a local connection? Is there any recent or planned local or national PR that will alert people to look out for it? What online presence do you have? Will your author website promote this store as a stockist? What about your social media? Do you have any events planned? Are you interested in holding an in-store event—and if so, would you bring your own audience? The better you have prepared possible questions in advance, the more confident and competent you will be in-store.

Choose Your Target

Start with the shop that makes you feel most confident of success: the one at which you are a regular customer, or the one whose clientele is the best match for your book. Once you've found success in one, you'll have more confidence to approach another, so be kind to yourself and pick off the easiest target first.

Pinpoint the Most Appropriate Staff Member

Phone the store, check out its website, or ask at a preliminary visit for the name of the staff member who is responsible for buying in stock. That way you can go straight to the person who has the most power to say yes to your proposition—and you won't embarrass yourself by giving your full pitch to someone who is only there for the day as cover for someone off sick, or who is about to move to a new job in a different store the next day. Make the first approach by email, so your target person can consider your proposal when it suits them and consult colleagues for their opinion if desired before responding.

Make an Appointment in Advance of Your Visit

Yes, you may get lucky and find that your target person is on the till if you pitch up at the store unannounced—but on the other hand, they will be there on duty to serve customers, and may not have the time to spare or the inclination to chat to authors who turn up unannounced.

And if they're happy to make an appointment, it shows they're already open to the idea of buying your book, so you can go into the meeting feeling you're already off to a good start. Social media expert and ALLi author Tim Lewis recommends following store managers on LinkedIn.

Have a Dummy Run

Be your own mystery shopper. If you're not already familiar with the bookstore, visit it beforehand, familiarize yourself with its layout, its opening hours, its website, its event program, and its typical customers. That way you'll be able to speak more knowledgeably and convincingly about why your book is a good fit for this particular store. Your research may even give you ideas for your meeting: for example, a proposal based on the success of a recent event held there.

Act the Part

Before you set foot in the store for your appointment, mentally prepare yourself to behave appropriately: be polite, professional, pleasant, and respectful. Stand tall and put your shoulders back—it'll relax you and make you feel and look more confident. Adopt a genuine smile, as if you're pleased to be there and to meet your contact (well, you are, aren't you?). Be ready to shake hands, or exchange bows, or whatever other gesture is the body language of the business-like in your country. Remember that the impression you make on first meeting will also be taken as an indicator of how well you'd perform at an in-store event. Obviously it would be impractical and prohibitively expensive to visit every store if you're planning a nationwide campaign, but going in person where you can will be much more effective than sending an email or posting a book and trusting to luck.

Offer Evidence

Accompany your elevator pitch for your book with evidence that it's not just you and your mother who think it's wonderful: flourish that ammunition you so carefully prepared before you came. You've probably got used to it by now, but when you show it all at once to fresh eyes, it will be impressive.

The importance of evidence means that you're unlikely to get your first book stocked the minute you publish it. Yes, bookstores like to stock some books that are hot off the press, but they will naturally be cautious about a new book by a new author with no track record. They also consistently stock books that have not been recently published, provided they will bring in a steady stream of sales. So bide your time until you have strong evidence to show them that your first book will be good for their store – and when the time comes for your second, third, fourth, etc, you will be in a stronger position with an established track record.

Be Passionate but Practical

No one can be as passionate about a book as its author, nor as knowledgeable, and you're in a unique position to answer questions about it. But make sure you listen to your contact's questions and respond to them, rather than treating the meeting as an opportunity to perform a soliloquy. Try to view the book from your potential stockist's perspective, and answer any questions, which are more likely to be about the practicalities of processing orders than about what inspired you to write the book in the first place. And if you are asked that kind of question, take heart—it's a buying signal! You've convinced your contact it's worth giving your book shelf space, so now you can concentrate on overcoming any obstacles to sealing the deal—sale or return arrangements, discounts, payment methods, and the like.

Follow the Buyer's Lead

If the buyer says yes, fantastic! Make sure you then go on to fulfil the agreed obligations, delivering the agreed number of books (if they're buying direct from you rather than from your distributor), promptly collecting unsold copies if you've agreed on sale or return, and submitting paperwork efficiently as required. Then move on to target your next most likely store.

Don't expect your buyer to take a whole case of your books straight away though. Most buyers will test the water with a small number of copies—think low single figures—and come back for more if those sell. So don't be disappointed. Have faith in your book—and try to hasten those first sales by promoting the store as a new stockist, via your website, social media, etc.

If the buyer doesn't make an immediate decision, accept that they need more time and ask what the next step should be—should you phone or email, or call in at a certain time, or leave it to them to contact you? Don't apply pressure or be at all ungracious. At least they haven't given you an outright no, and that's a good thing! Any reasons for hesitating are likely to be sound and considered. They may want to consult colleagues, to consider how it might fit in with other books ordered in that genre, or even to take the time to read the book in person. Wait until the agreed time to follow up your meeting, and when you do so, do it courteously by the agreed method, such as email rather than phone.

And if a buyer does like your book, they're likely not only to stock a couple of copies, but also to actively hand sell it, talking enthusiastically to customers whom they think would also enjoy it.

Nic Bottomley, co-proprietor of Mr B's Emporium in Bath, England, says:

> We will actively promote a book we like. A book needs to sell at least four copies year as the economic minimum to earn its place on the shelf, whereas our bestseller will shift six or seven hundred copies a year. But a bookseller will cut a bit of slack if there is a book they just want to stock regardless of sales, such as favourite classics.

But if the buyer does say no, at least they've given you the chance to pitch. Accept defeat graciously. Try to assess whether there was anything you did wrong, or whether it's simply the case that the book isn't a good fit for the store, and once you've gleaned anything there is to learn from the experience, move on. There are plenty more bookstores out there, and at least now you have a ready-made contact for when you're ready to go in and pitch your next book.

Unless you're a onebook author, the key objective is to build a long-term partnership with booksellers, not just to get a one-off encounter. As a sideline, fantasy author Thomas Shepherd is an illustrator, producing beautiful pen-and-ink drawings of bookstores and heritage buildings for sale as prints and cards. He took a long-term attitude to his local indie bookstore: "My books are now in stock at Books and Ink, but that was after a year of building a relationship and supplying cards. The moral of the story is to build a slow, strong relationship with bookstores."

Whatever you do, don't take rejection personally. Remember there are so many books out there vying for the same shelf space as you in that store, and only a tiny percentage can physically fit. The buyers who curate that stock are experienced, specialist professionals, and they make their decisions for sound commercial reasons. It's disappointing, of course, if you're a longstanding regular customer of a particular bookstore that refuses to stock your book. If it's any consolation, the buyer probably feels bad about making that decision, but, at the end of the day, they have their job to do, and their objectives are different to yours.

Say Thank You

Finally, whatever the outcome, thank your contact for their time and consideration, and make sure you have left contact details for future reference (these should be in your AI sheet, but you may also want to leave a card or bookmark if you have one), and leave promptly. Lingering in the shop afterwards to browse or even buy a book would be courteous and wise.

The Numbers Game

Assuming that in theory you can be successful in getting a potential bookstore to stock your books, in chapter 11 we'll look at the financial considerations surrounding your deal. But first a look at the logistics of running a book launches in a bookstore.

10

BOOKSTORE BOOK LAUNCHES
LAUNCHES AND EVENTS

Bookstores often welcome indie author events as a way of bringing in extra business and offering their customers an interesting and exclusive experience. "We are finding bookshops ordering indie books, but the majority of orders are still online," says Andy Bromley of IngramSpark. "We see, however, that there is value in bookshops using authors to create experiences which online book retailers cannot replicate. The bookshops which are thriving are doing this – engaging with the community rather than relying on passing trade for business," says Andy Bromley.

If you're organizing or taking part in an in-store event it can make sense to use the consignment system. This means your books are stocked at the store during your event, and possibly shortly before and shortly afterwards, and sold through their tills. In effect, it will have stocked your books for a day.

While that may seem less satisfactory than having them in stock for longer, if you manage your event well and demonstrate strong demand and interest on the day, the store management may be persuaded to stock your books long term. And if it doesn't, well, at least you've had a glorious day of being the star of the bookstore, which, with strategic use of good event photography, you can use to generate further useful PR via your website and social media.

So what kind of in-store event might work for your book, and what do you need to do to set one up?

Book Launches

Holding an in-store launch is a great way to celebrate the birth of your book. However, do not expect the bookstore staff to run it for you. You will need to treat it as your own party, at your own expense, providing the refreshments, decorations, advance publicity, and invitations to ensure you have plenty of guests show up. Even if the bookstore kindly advertises the event for you, don't expect it to field many guests from the general public. That will be down to you. To help raise your credibility and build your long-term relationship with the store staff, do all you can to bring in everyone you know. Even better, see if you can persuade them all to buy books on the night, via the store, especially if you know they're likely to buy them anyway.

A good launch, well run, can be exhausting and expensive. Don't expect to recover your costs in profits from your book sales. But do be on the lookout to extract every benefit you can from the event, from sharing advance publicity on your website, in the local media, and on social media, to post-event news stories. You may find it leads to other event opportunities such as signings at other stores or talks at local libraries or special interest shops.

Some bookstores prefer to run events outside of their normal opening hours so as not to interfere with trading patterns or sales of the rest of their stock. In stores that have very little room to move, they may even prefer to host events at a different venue away from the shop, though endorsing it from the shop and promoting it as their event. Don't be offended if they suggest either of these alternatives; just graciously accept what you're offered and make the best of it.

Novelist Sandy Osborne offers an encouraging case study of the launch of her debut novel *Girl Cop* at her local store:

Organizing a launch isn't dissimilar to planning a wedding. Invitations, wine, glasses hire, helium balloons (color coded to match the cover), photographer, and flowers for a special guest.

I even managed to persuade the manager to let me have a window display—positioning a full-sized model of me, in uniform, outside the shop, along with numerous posters/copies of the cover and a small table with a few books displayed on it.

I sent out invites to everyone I know. As the launch was going to be after Christmas, every Christmas card I sent included an invite! I recruited four friends to "meet and greet" and run the bar. I handed out fliers to everyone I thought looked within my readership, from the checkout ladies in the supermarket to those queuing behind me! I looked out my old Dr Marten boots from the attic and organized my table display for the night.

I texted and emailed everyone in my contacts lists both before Christmas and again shortly before the event. I didn't ask for RSVPs—I just crossed my fingers! I also managed to get a piece in the local paper.

Over 180 people turned out to help me celebrate its final release on a cold January evening—and I sold over 100 books!

While a strong launch clearly requires hard work and is more likely to cost you money than turn a profit, it's a great way to impress bookstore staff, as well as to bolster your own ego and local status as a successful author.

The store staff were so impressed with Sandy Osborne's achievement—"the most well-attended local author launch in my 25 years as a bookseller," said the senior member of staff—that they hosted the launch of its sequel during normal store hours, and continued to stock both books long term.

Scottish author Wendy Jones made a similar impact with the launch event for her first novel in the Dundee branch of Waterstones. She said:

> Since the launch, Killer's Countdown has continued to sell well. It has good product placement and has been displayed in the store window. It is always displayed cover out, rather than spine out, and it is on several tables throughout the store. I cannot thank Waterstones' Dundee branch enough for the way in which they have promoted it.
>
> However, the story does not stop there. The book is also stocked in several other Waterstones stores in Scotland. Following the success of my partnership with Waterstones, I approached other bookstores. CLC Bookstore in Dundee is also stocking my book. In partnership with them, we put on a Focus on Fiction week with my book as the main focus. Several weeks later, it was still in the window of the store. The Emporium, an independent bookstore in Cromarty, is also stocking it.

English thriller writer Edward Parry explains his smart tactic for adding value to his signing event at his local bookshop:

> For my debut thriller, *Golem*, I tied my first signing at WHSmith in Tamworth with my visits to local schools, so some of their pupils came. In all, I found the experience incredibly positive, and the staff were encouraging and seemed genuinely pleased to see me. Some even bought a copy of *Golem* for themselves. I would recommend anyone who is unsure about bookstore events just to try it. I will definitely be doing it again in as many stores as I can.

Post-launch Events

Launching a new book is one good excuse for an in-store event, but there are many more. Forward-thinking bookstores whose business model identifies them as a cultural center of the community are always looking for authors to stage in-store events. It's much easier for them to involve local authors, regardless of how they are published (and cheaper, if otherwise they might be expected to pay travel expenses for guest authors from afar).

Some stores even aim at an event every night—an ambitious plan that will take some feeding. So don't be shy. Any bookstore tasked with filling its events schedule should be glad to hear from you, provided you approach them with a well-considered plan appropriate to their clientele.

Bookstores often like to tie in with national and international events:

- anniversaries or centenaries that are likely to be in the public eye
- Olympic Games and other sporting championships
- national bookseller-driven campaigns, e.g. in the US, the annual Independent Bookstore Day; in Australia, National Bookstore Day; in Canada, Authors for Indies Day; and in the UK, Independent Booksellers' Week and the Books Are My Bag campaign
- Publisher-driven campaigns, e.g. World Book Day and World Book Night.

For all of these events, bookstores will welcome suggestions. They may be planning special events and activities that are likely to increase the demand for authors in-store. While this doesn't necessarily mean they'll be more likely to stock your book at other times, it's worth investigating early to see whether there are ways that you can become involved in any events that are a good fit for your books and genre.

If you are able to engineer an interesting event, either on your own or with one or more other authors, you may be able to persuade a bookstore to host it, especially if you promise to bring your own audience, i.e. book-buying customers. Add interest and value for the bookstore – and manpower and moral support for yourself – by joining forces with other local authors.

In an interesting piece of lateral thinking, alternative history thriller writer Alison Morton joined forces with trade-published steampunk author Liesel Schwarz, to build the audiences for both of their books via joint in-store events:

Although we both write alternative worlds, Liesel with steampunk, me with alternative history, we obviously share a sense of the offbeat.

Liesel and I met through the Romantic Novelists' Association. Our books have boy-meets-girl emotional relationships, which is the crux of the matter for the RNA. As we write in speculative settings, world-building is at the forefront of our writing craft. It goes beyond setting, as we have to create a whole new world, although the characters in our books remain very human. You can imagine the discussions we have!

Although Liesel has been hailed as the new high-priestess of steampunk by The Independent newspaper, and I've had a fair bit of success in historical and adventure fiction, neither of us is a household name, so we decided to band together to do some author talks.

We knew were a good match for a joint event: similar enough subject areas, both outgoing communicators with successful books. Of course, having the mighty Random House PR officer helped in terms of clout; we were in The Independent's "i" newspaper's diary under "cultural events not to be missed"! It was also a great opportunity to draw attention to my newly launched novel Aurelia, the fourth in my Roma Nova series.

Keep a lookout for other authors' events in your area that might inspire you to formulate your own ideas. Go along to them, see what works well and what not so well, and learn from their experience. They will also provide good networking opportunities for you.

In-store events will usually include at least one reading by an author, so make sure you hone your skills on reading your books aloud. ALLi news editor and Author Member Dan Holloway, an award-winning performance poet and author, explains why getting the reading, the timing, and the delivery right are so important:

I get up in front of people and say my words a lot. Both poetry and prose. I also run a lot of events. The combination gives a fascinating insight into what makes a reading work well.

The really interesting thing is that, from both sides, three minutes works incredibly well if you are putting together a series of readings.

For an organizer, with a tight schedule you have very carefully crafted so as to do right by audience, venue, and every author with their individual needs, you need people to stick to the time you have given them. Not doing so is, quite simply, rude. And three minutes of reading means five minutes per person, once you've introduced them, people have applauded, and everyone's done the shimmy to the front and back again. (When you see a time that says you're reading at 7.45 and the next person's on at 7.50, and the organizer has said you have three minutes, they really mean three minutes and these changeover rituals are why.) And five minutes is an easy time to work with.

For both of you, though, there's another reason three minutes works. And that reason is the most important thing about the whole event. Your audience. What do you both want for your audience? You want them to go away and tell everyone about these amazing writers they heard. And to just have to find the books of the ones they really loved—the books they didn't walk out with under their arm.

Which brings me to another incidental point about multi-author events and three minutes. The thing with such wonderful diverse events is that everyone will love something. And no one will love everything. And that's how it should be. And everyone's prepared to sit through three minutes of something they're not into to wait for the stuff they might really love. 27 minutes—not so much. People might leave. Because of you. That's the audience you've annoyed, and for that reason the organizer, too. And also those fellow authors who never got heard by people who might have loved them.

Anyway, back to the real reason for three minutes.

Three minutes is the standard length allowed for readings at a poetry slam, because it maximizes the author's ability to demonstrate their skills without pushing the reader's attention span to breaking. And this holds for prose as much as it does for poetry.

A great reading isn't three minutes plus "this is how I came to write the book, this is what happened previously and what is facing my character now"; it's three minutes including that. A self-contained piece needs little or no introduction.

So the perfect set? By all means give us your elevator pitch, a really witty or catchy intro, say 15–20 seconds, and allow the audience five seconds to laugh, squirm, applaud uproariously. Then read for two and a half minutes, thank everyone, and wave your book as you leave in triumph.

11

FINANCIAL CONSIDERATIONS
MAKING A PROFIT

The next logical question is whether the economics make sense. Is it worthwhile for both you as the supplier and for the bookstore as the customer interface to stock and sell your book?

Is It Potentially Profitable for All Parties?

Let's recap: you've got a book that is beautifully written, professionally presented, and a great fit for the clientele of the bookstore that you are targeting. Sounds good enough? Think again. Unless you're able to offer booksellers a viable profit margin, they may still turn you down. Remember, there are plenty of other books, authors, and publishers vying for the same shelf space. If they offer a better business proposition than you do, you may still fail to win over the bookseller. It has to be not only worth the bookseller's while to stock it, but be as valuable a contributor to profit as the best contenders.

A classic newbie error is to neglect to include in your calculations a substantial profit margin for the bookseller. Some authors seem outraged that the bookseller wants to take a slice of the pie at all. Why does the bookseller need a cut of your retail price? It's called capitalism, and that's how it works. Why do booksellers need such a high percentage? Just look at the issue from the other side of the till: book margins are the oxygen of any bookstore business. Booksellers stray from these established margins at the peril of their store's viability. Just think of your book as a tenant in the shop, having to pay its rent and other overheads: its share of the lighting, heating, staff wages, and so on, all of which are effectively the running costs of its little space on the shelf.

When you look at it that way, the bookstore's cut seems less of an imposition and more of a bargain. I often wonder at the care booksellers put into selling each book for such a tiny amount, and how they stay in business—and stay cheerful—at all.

The industry standard bare minimum a bookseller will expect is 30%, but 35–40% is more usual, while big chains offering prime spots in multiple stores may ask as much as 60%. For self-published authors operating on a print-on-demand basis, in which the print cost per book is higher than traditional offset litho, such a high percentage can be difficult to accommodate without making a loss. This dilemma is often the determining factor for indies when deciding to turn their backs on bookstore sales.

Remember to factor your time and travel costs into your dealings with bookstores. Coupled with a narrow margin, the proposition can seem distinctly unattractive.

Your attitude towards bookshops may also be partly determined by your personal experience of them. British novelist Jane Steen, recently returned from living in the US, describes her conscious decision to ignore bookstores in her business model:

> How relevant are bookstores in a world where (a) more than 50% of print books are sold online (b) no bookstore can ever stock more than a fraction of the available books and (c) many people don't have a bookstore near them anyway, especially in the US. I have to admit I don't bother trying to sell to bookstores – it seems like a lot of trouble when the same amount of time can be spent on an online advertising campaign that might sell 500 units.

I understand the reasons people love them but somehow in the last few years I lost my own love of bookstores, probably because I was living in the Chicago suburbs, where bookstores were becoming places that pushed toys and tat in your face rather than books. Big anonymous places where the only books that seemed to matter to them were the bestsellers. The real book lovers seemed to be in the superb public libraries which is where most of the author events were held.

See ALLi's short guide **Your Book in Worldwide Libraries** for advice on how to build better relationships with libraries: SelfPublishingAdvice.org/bookshop.

Returning to the topic of bookstores, it's down to you and your negotiating skills to decide your attitude to profit margins. Some authors are so keen to get their books on the bookstore shelf that they'll accept orders on a breakeven basis, or even at a loss. But you are not obliged to give the bookseller more than you wish to. You can walk away from any deal.

If you are one of those who wishes to get your books stocked at any cost, will it favor you to offer a higher discount? There's no firm answer there—it depends on the nature of your book. If it's appealing to a clear niche market in which you have little competition, the value of your book to the bookseller is higher than if you are writing in a large genre along with many other authors. If the bookseller can feed the same demand with books at 40% or 50% or 60%, they'll need to have a very good reason to stock your book at a lower profit. However, if you're able to convince the bookseller that your book, at a 30% margin, will sell three times as many as one with the same retail price at 60% profit, you have an advantage. It's not rocket science; it's simple arithmetic.

If booksellers won't take your low-margin book as part of standard stock, they may still be prepared to order it for customers who ask for it—a response to the "pull" of the customers, rather than their own "push" to sell it. Booksellers aim to please their customers and pride themselves on going the extra mile. I spoke to a bookseller recently who was placing special orders for books that would earn her literally a penny profit, because she valued that customer and regarded it as a special service. Let's hope the customer appreciates her dedication to duty and buys plenty more books at a high margin to repay her kindness. But bear in mind that, when you're asking for a lower margin, you're really asking for your books to be subsidized by the books that are selling at a higher markup.

When setting the discount, it's easy to assume that the bookseller gets the whole of that amount. The situation is more complicated than that. Andy Bromley of IngramSpark explains:

> This really isn't specific to POD, it is part of the global supply chain of books. This is the same with litho printing because it isn't the printing format but the difference between the retail discount and wholesale discount. It's complex because the wholesaler who supplies the bookstore may buy from another wholesaler. Discount is agreed between the retailer and wholesaler on a contractual basis and there are variables that come into play that determine the discounts (volume, location, size, negotiation skills). Large multinational publishers might have their own distribution chain because they have critical mass, which is why they can beat indies (economy of scale is 95% of it).

It's not possible for the indie author (or any other kind of publisher) to know exactly which bookstore gets what, because these amounts are individual and private contracts involving the distributor, wholesaler, and bookseller. But it is clear that the setup is more complex than it seems at first glance.

Not all booksellers can negotiate the same deals with publishers, distributors, or wholesalers. Some big chains of bookstores have much more buying power than others, simply because they can shift books in much higher numbers.

The way the marketplace operates varies around the world. Author-publisher Ritesh Kala describes the scenario in India:

The discount received by bookstores mainly is the result of their own negotiation power. The large chains can get a discount as high as 40–50%, whereas the small independents are happy with 25–30%. The other issue is that not every small store can buy directly from the large distributors, so they are supplied by other sub-distributors who keep a margin in there as well. However, the overall discount received by bookstores is always dependent on the discount offered by the publisher to the main distributor. The large ones can give the same distributor about 10% lower discount as compared to the smaller publishers, and still reach many more bookstores.

That bigger markup may make the difference between ordering and not ordering your book. When selling via a distributor, the author, incidentally, gets the same compensation or royalty set up front however a bookstore orders your book.

So, although you may be offering 40%, for example, by the time the other parties have been involved in the chain, the bookstore may receive only about 20%. Fundamentally, although the situation may look simple to you, the author, when you set your discount in the different territories, the true situation can be more complex, with slices of that discount divided up between whatever distributors, sub-distributors, or wholesalers there are in the chain. Theoretically, from both the author's and the bookstore's perspective, the more direct the better—although the bookstores presumably accept the reduced discount as a trade-off for other helpful benefits from their distributor or wholesaler, such as being able to order books from multiple authors and multiple publishers on a single invoice, and practical concessions such as free delivery and collection, and favorable payment terms.

Therefore, no matter how you feel about offering a discount, don't rush to accuse any bookseller of greed, because they may be getting far less than you assume. In any case, it's up to you to set the discount, and no bookstore or distributor can extract from you more discount than you are prepared to allow. You just need to bear in mind that the more generous a discount you allow, the more attractive the bookseller will find your book will be—though if it's a book that a bookseller doesn't expect to be able to sell in the store, even 100% discount isn't going to be an attractive option. If the book doesn't sell, the profit will be zero, and the bookseller would be better off having a profit-generating book in that space on the shelf.

Clearly the fewer parties involved in the transaction, the more profit for both the indie author and the bookseller, with the proviso that the bookseller prefers to deal with multiple authors via one distributor. Distributors also usually offer a key benefit that the sole trader indie author would be unable to offer: free delivery, even for an order of a single book.

Publishing via IngramSpark or Lightning Source enables indie authors to get books into bookstores via the main distributors, because Ingram has an established relationship as their supplier. This is one of many reasons we recommend indie authors to publish with IngramSpark.

However, it doesn't solve the issue of diminishing profits when more parties are involved in the distribution chain.

Ingram Book Group's service, ipage, is an attempt to cut out the middle-men. It enables bookstores to order any books from its catalogue directly, for speedy, free delivery, on all orders of any size. None of the books in the catalogue are identified as self-published, which is also helpful.

ipage is being rolled out globally and in any of the growing number of territories in which it is operational (currently US, Canada, UK and Australia) any indie author who has published via either Lightning Source or IngramSpark may set up a free ipage account.

If you do this, your print on demand books will always be shown as in stock and available to booksellers, and will always be promptly despatched, with 48 hours as the target timescale for paperback titles.

Bookstores need to have an ipage account for this to work. In the US and Canada, where booksellers tend to be more familiar with Ingram, many have been quick to embrace this new service. In territories where Ingram is less well-known, a bookstore may need to be persuaded to deal with an additional distributor to their usual choice.

In return, they will almost always earn a bigger discount by ordering an indie book via ipage than via any other distribution route.

If you suspect you're dealing with a bookstore that hasn't yet become acquainted with ipage, do explain it to them. They may assume the only way to order your author-published books is in small consignments and may well thank you for the introduction, as they have much to gain from it. Key selling points of ipage for them is that it's free to open an account and they don't need to pay anything until they order books.

More information about ipage: IngramContent.com/ipage

Are You Offering Sale or Return?

Besides speed of delivery and ease of ordering, another significant concern for the bookseller is whether or not you are offering sale or return. To spell out exactly what this means for you, the author, if you tick the box to offer sale or return, it means that a bookstore may effectively order copies of your book speculatively, without a commitment to selling them. Thus, if your book doesn't sell after a set period, the bookstore may return it to the supplier for a full refund, leaving you to cover the production cost without the sale to offset it.

Think long and hard before ticking that box. While you may think that you would be happy to write off the cost of an occasional return, if it guaranteed bookstore shelf space for your book, doing so exposes you to much greater risk. Just supposing you pulled off a particularly good piece of marketing, leading to increased awareness of your book nationwide, or one of your blog posts or tweets went viral—there could be a surge in demand from bookstores whose radar you'd suddenly appeared on.

There could feasibly be hundreds or thousands of orders, but without any guarantee of sales. If the marketing hubbub dies down very quickly, most or all of the books ordered at its peak might be returned unsold, leaving you responsible for a massive debt. Small publishing houses have gone out of business this way.

Novelist Chris Longmuir reports on her near miss with sale or return:

> One thing I have learned to look out for is the sale or return policy expected by booksellers. I was caught once when Foyles wanted to return books they had ordered for Crimefest (literary event). However, I was able to body-swerve that one because I had given no such agreement. It did alert me to the problem though, because the markup on paperback books is minimal after the discount and postage is applied, and if returns require to be financed I would be seriously out of pocket. All my invoices now have a statement at the bottom saying "All sales final: No sale or return policy", and so far it has worked.

If having their stock underwritten seems to give bookstores an unfair advantage over the individual author, that's too bad—the system is designed to sustain viable bookstores, not to balance authors' bank accounts.

But do not despair: as mentioned earlier, deciding not to play the sale or return game won't necessarily eliminate you from any bookstore interest. Bookstores will almost always buy in a book to fulfil a specific customer order, even if it's not on sale or return, because they have effectively already sold the book, therefore there won't be a return.

By the way, it's worth noting that, if you have approached a bookstore in person to try to place your books, the bookseller may not realize that your books will be available via the standard distributors, so do go out of your way to make that clear to them when making your pitch. This detail should be included in your AI sheet too. Although obviously you should always respect the bookseller's experience and knowledge, they are not infallible or all-knowing, so if you're sure of your ground, be prepared to gently inform or politely correct a bookseller if need be.

When novelist Rosalind Minett was told adamantly by small local bookstores that they could not accept her books, she says:

> I just phoned IngramSpark, who confirmed that the little bookstores who would only take copies from me, not order, were mistaken. Ingrams DO distribute through Gardners every day, also Bertrams and Askews.

However, most bookstores will prefer to order through their usual supplier rather than dealing directly with the author. A bookstore typically places orders every day with their regular supplier, through a single, streamlined account. For every new supplier e.g a single author dealing directly, a new account must be set up, which means more paperwork for the store, and it can also considerably slow down the process of restocking once your initial supply sells out. It's also requires more admin from you, the author – not only must you deliver the books in a timely fashion, you must also submit an invoice at the same time and manage the accounting side of the business.

If you do agree to supply a store directly on a sale or return basis, it is your responsibility to keep track of when you delivered stock, to agree the period of the return option (typically three months), and to collect unsold stock at the end of that period. If you do not collect your stock within the agreed time, the store is within its rights to dispose of them as they think fit, whether by a reduced-price sale or disposing of them elsewhere.

Remember, for the vast majority of booksellers, the bulk of their business is not done directly with the author, or with the self-publishing sector, so they are still on a learning curve. Take the opportunity to help ease them along that curve, but only when it really is appropriate and you're sure of your facts.

The Personal Touch

Even when your books can be provided easily through the normal channels, booksellers may sometimes seem to prefer to deal with the author direct, as I've found myself when placing my books in my nearest stockists. Sometimes I've even been paid in cash from the till for my books. I think they appreciate that you are trying to build a relationship with them, and they welcome your presence, they're likely to be saying good things about you and your books to their customers.

Thriller writer Anne Stormont reports:

> I've had a similar experience in local bookstores in Scotland: they want me to provide the copies directly, even though they're available through their usual distributor as I went with Ingram Spark.

If that's how they prefer to operate, consider whether it's better to go with the flow, even though by this point you may realize it's much more convenient and cost-effective for you to have your books part of that consolidated order and shipment rather than visiting regularly to replenish their stocks or collect returns (if you choose to do so). Incidentally, if you're supplying directly by hand, offering sale or return is less risky, because you know the potential number of returns is small, and that the returned stock will be in better condition—possibly re-saleable—than if submitted via delivery drivers or postal services.

It may be simply an economic consideration, if the bookseller buys via a wholesaler who is taking their own cut of the discount first. Thus, the bookseller will make more per book if buying directly from you at the discount you'd offer via your distributor, even when adding in to the equation the value of the extra time and trouble it takes to process your invoice and payment.

But there may also just be an element of curiosity. They probably don't often get to speak to authors in person, and they may be glad to have this opportunity, even though you're not (yet) a household name.

Hand delivery also gives you the opportunity to build strong relationships with the booksellers, the chance to chat to customers, and regular occasions to remind the bookseller of your existence and to update them with your news. English novelist Hattie Holden Edmonds told me that it's one of her favorite times of the week when she cycles around her stockists in her hometown of Whitstable on the Kentish coast to take in new stock. While not all of us have the luxury of being able to maintain supplies without the need for petrol, parking, or postage costs, her attitude is inspiring.

Why, then, don't booksellers want to buy all indie books directly from the authors? The time required to deal with separate individuals for each book may be one factor, but also the booksellers may be getting other benefits from the distributor, such as free postage for delivery and returns, the ability to stock a book at a strategic time to suit their customers rather than timed around your visits, or prolonged payment terms, such as 60 or 90 days credit.

"Standard practice for bookstores is to pay 30 days after the end of the month in which a book has been supplied," says Peter Snell, a recently retired bookseller. "Indie authors need to be aware of this. It can be annoying to be chased for payment in the same month the book was supplied."

The Bottom Line—Is It Profitable for You?

In the final analysis, the economics of selling your books through bookstores are complex, and partly outside of the author–publisher's control. As the author, you must pay great attention to setting your side of the bargain, with careful consideration of selling prices, discounts, and terms and conditions (especially sale or return). Many authors decide the prospect of selling through bookstores is so fraught with complexity, risk, and dubious profitability that the game is not worth the candle. On the other hand, those who reject this route cut themselves off from any potential readers who dislike ordering online and prefer to order through their local bookstores, whether for moral or ethical reasons, or because they are technophobes.

If having read this far you've decided that selling your books through bookstores simply would not repay the time, effort, and costs, it's up to you to make the decision not to pursue that route. Bear in mind, though, that other motives may justify your continuing pursuit of bookstores. Nicola Solomon, CEO of the Society of Authors, counsels: "Don't do anything unless it fulfils one of the three Ps: profit, pleasure or publicity." As ever with indie publishing, you call the shots, and whatever decision feels right to you is the right decision for you. Don't let anyone tell you otherwise.

But before you give up on bookstores entirely, note that there are other ways of selling your books through bookstores, and of gaining a presence and raising your profile before readers, which may be more profitable and desirable, and which you should not dismiss without due consideration. In Chapter 12 we'll describe these other possibilities.

12

OTHER WAYS OF SELLING PRINT BOOKS

Even when a bookstore is unwilling to order your books to stock and sell in the conventional manner, it may still be willing to sell your books. We saw in an earlier chapter that bookstores are willing to place special orders. To make the most of this opportunity, include in the call to action on the book pages on your website the option of ordering from a local bookshop, quoting the ISBNs to help the bookseller find your books on his supplier's database.

Consignment deals are negotiated in advance at a local level between you and the store management. You take in an agreed number of books, they add them to their stock for the duration of your event, and you take away the unsold ones afterwards, which they remove from their stock. Customers won't notice any difference, and the store will still receive the agreed profit margin, but no distributor or wholesaler is involved.

You then invoice the store for the books it has sold on your behalf, at the agreed discount.

Selling Print Rights to a Third Party

Thinking laterally, there is another way to sell your books through bookstores, without worrying about profit margins and discounts and without the expense or effort of any of the activities outlined in this and the previous two chapters, and that is to sell your paperback rights to a third party, retaining only the ebook rights (which have a greater margin and requiring lower investment).

This position has worked very well for the likes of Hugh Howey, who was offered a deal for his ebook and print rights. He preferred to retain ebook rights, on the basis that there was nothing a publisher could do for his ebooks that he couldn't do himself. However, for print, he was happy to trade control for the greater power for the greater presence in bookstores that publishers could provide through their established channels than he could engineer for himself.

This is also a smart way in which to get your book translated and into bookstores in other countries. Orna Ross, ALLi director and author of the book *How Authors Sell Publishing Rights*, explains the choices and challenges inherent in this option, if you want to seek it out.

Traditionally—before the dawn of the ebook—the right to produce a book in a new print edition was referred to in a contract as reprint rights. Reprints come in a variety of sizes and shapes. They might include deluxe editions, large-print editions, illustrated editions, hardcover, and other special-format versions of a book. Most commonly, however, the term reprint rights refers to paperback reprint rights.

Authors and publishers choose whether a book will be published first in ebook, hardcover, or paperback. For some books, especially genre books (romance, Western, science fiction, and mystery), the first and primary format is paperback. For author–publishers, the primary format tends to be ebook and in-print, via print-on-demand. But many books are also initially distributed in a hardcover edition.

Traditionally, paperbacks were always treated as reprints of hardcover books in this way; now, trade publishers tend to purchase paperback and hardcover rights at the same time, removing paperback from the category of subsidiary right "reprints".

What is happening now is that paperback houses generally offer royalties of less than 10% gross and may also try to get you to part with ebook royalties at just 15–25% of net receipts, a poor deal for indie authors used to selling direct to readers at up to 70% commission.

ALLi would argue that, when paperback rights are licensed by an indie author to another publisher, the paperback rights become a subsidiary right, and you might want to start the negotiation with the usual subsidiary split: 50/50 publisher/author. How this will go will depend on how much they want your book. And it's worth saying that no publisher will be interested in print rights (or translation or any other rights) unless you have already proven your ability to sell a lot of books in ebook format.

Your pitch will vary depending on what rights you're looking to sell and whether you are pitching by email or in person. Either way, once you've done your market research and have your content in place (book description, review materials, etc., as well as the book itself), a good pitch is all about presentation.

Whether you're pitching to agents or publishers, think about their needs and don't be afraid to propose suggestions that might help them. As an author–publisher, you have to convince the buyer of the quality of the writing, your dedication as a writer, and your ability to reach readers.

Make your pitch easy to navigate, so people can absorb information quickly. In the words of Joseph Pulitzer, "Put it before them briefly so they will read it, clearly so they will appreciate it, picturesquely so they will remember it and, above all, accurately so they will be guided by its light."

Here are some useful tips to bear in mind when pitching print rights:

- **Research:** Thoroughly research the agency or publisher, getting into their skin and thinking about ways your book enhances their offering, extends the discoverability of their other books, and helps them meet their goals.

- **Professional:** Whether pitching to an agent who can help you sell your rights, or directly to a publisher, your presentation should be simple, clean, and professional, i.e. in the proper file format with the appropriate tone and voice. Copy should be clean and demonstrate sufficient knowledge and skill. Avoid gimmicks like crazy fonts or pictures; these only detract from your pitch.

- **Clarity:** Make it clear what is available to read now and what you hope the agent or publisher will achieve for you. Say why you write and who you identify as your audience. If you have been trade-published or have had an agent before, give details.

- **Honest dealing:** No hiding, subterfuge, or trying to put one over on anyone. If this is a multiple submission, say so.

- **Passion:** Be passionate about your work. Don't boast or drone on and on, but don't be afraid to show enthusiasm and tout your success. Practice a way of doing this without overselling or sounding immodest.

- **Success:** List your achievements, presenting your ideas and your work clearly, simply, and without hyperbole. If you have stats or analytics, prizes or sales points, here is the place to share them. Say what you have already published, what you have already written, and what you see as long-term and achievable goals. Give examples of your success throughout the entire pitch.

- **Openness:** Listen to what the agent or publisher is saying and ask follow-up questions. See what you can learn. Show true and sincere passion while being open to feedback.

- **Language:** Think about the language you use to describe your books and your ambitions. One agent we know recommends saying "our" and "we" early on in the pitch, already subtly including yourself in the agent or publisher's team.

- **Questions:** Anticipate likely questions and prepare your answers. Make a list of questions to ask, and do ask them.

- **Strengths:** Highlight your strengths and where you add value. If you've got specialist skills that are rare to find, or something that no one else can offer (and most of us have), tell the agent or publisher. Many writers find this challenging. Practice and get better.

- **Be yourself, warts and all:** Don't be afraid to admit to gaps or weaknesses. Relax and smile, be friendly, and don't be afraid to crack the odd joke. Keep things light and be genuinely interested in the people you're pitching to. People always want to work with people they like; people like people who like them.

It bears mentioning that you need to know when the rules can be bent. Sometimes the conventional method of doing things is less effective than getting creative. If your pitch still holds true to Pulitzer's advice, and these general guidelines, it doesn't need to lockstep in line with all the "rules." There are no rules; there is only what works.

Don't be quirky or different just for the sake of it, however. If you choose to color outside the lines, it needs to be consistent with and illustrative of your pitch.

For a detailed consideration of rights issues, read ALLi's guidebook *How Authors Sell Publishing Rights* by Orna A Ross.

Selling Print Books Online

And finally, a reminder that bookstores are not the only places to sell print books. Although the majority of books sold online are ebooks, online retailers offer an opportunity to make significant sales in print too.

Many readers who buy books online buy print. Marketing programs designed to promote ebooks may have a knock-on effect on the print sales too.

Through its Self-Publishing 3.0 campaign ALLi encourages authors to have transactional websites and sell direct to readers. While this works very well for ebooks and audiobooks, which can be delivered at the push of a digital button, print is more unwieldy and costly of time and money.

If you are set up for print-on-demand with Amazon and Ingram, your books are automatically offered on any sites they have a relationship with, and shipping and fulfilment are sorted. As we've said in earlier chapters, the big perk is that you don't have to pack and post, or keep track of inventory. Drop shipping your own orders will take longer to deliver than sales through Amazon and is time consuming.

If you like the idea of having print books for sale on your site, but would like someone else to manage the fulfilment, Ingram's embryonic Aer.io service can help. It has limited availability at the time of writing, only available in the US, but the company has plans to expand the service. With Aer.io, the reader purchases the book on your site, and Ingram sends the book in an anonymous brown carton which doesn't indicate in any way that it didn't come from you.

Here are three other ways of selling direct that require you to manage the fulfilment from your own stock:

1. Use Paypal, WooCommerce or other merchant or ecommerce service to process orders via your website – expect to pay a fee per transaction.
2. Open an Amazon vendor account, with a link from your website, so that "your" shop is effectively hosted as part of their marketplace, but you would still need to manage the fulfilment.
3. Set up an Etsy.com store or similar, again accessed via a link from your website, through which you could also offer little

extras not possible through POD services, e.g. signed copies, bookmarks or other promotional material. Polish novelist Bjorn Larsson has used this effectively to sell signed copies of the hardback edition of his debut novel *Storytellers*, particularly for the pre-Christmas market.

Of course direct selling from your website brings its own challenges – not only physically fulfilling orders, but also factoring in variable postage costs and handling local tax and import issues.

Andy Bromley advises: "If selling overseas, wholesalers and distributors will deal with tax and customers for you. That is part of the value that they bring to the supply chain."

Some authors are up for the challenge. If you're expecting to sell print in large volumes from your own website, remember that bulk purchases will require you to store your books somewhere. Depending on your sales volume, you are likely to need a warehouse rather than just storing books in your home office. And you'll need to ensure that any warehouse you use can work seamlessly with your website's eCommerce platform, your printer, and your inventory management software.

You may also benefit from a transportation management system (TMS), also known as "shipping software", to automate the fulfilment process, from the order arriving in on your website to delivery to the reader's door through a courier like FedEx, UPS, etc. Such systems can help you to make the best selection based on your reader's location, simplifying and optimizing your fulfilment process, and saving on shipping expenses—a large part of your cost in this business model.

For this model to work, time and money wise, you need to establish a steady stream of sales in print, through advertising and other marketing methods, and have assistance in fulfilling and shipping orders. For most indie authors, this is not viable. Even those who sell large numbers of ebooks and audiobooks from their websites are happy to leave print fulfilment to the two big POD services, Amazon KDPP and IngramSpark.

13

HOW I DO IT
ALLI MEMBERS' BOOKSTORE EXPERIENCES

As evidence of how, with the right product, approach, and attitude, indie authors can indeed sell self-published books through bookstores, here are some encouraging case studies from ALLi members around the world.

Prue Batten, Australia: When I first published my local Dymocks store was absolutely fabulous. They ordered my books from Ingram because I was a local writer, stocked them on the front pedestal of the store, and they subsequently told me they sold more of that title than any other new-release author they had profiled.

When I became indie, I always said my books had to survive on their own merits—no consignment: independent orders from bookstores and readers only. It worked!

Dymocks in Tasmania is a lateral-thinking store with a tremendous attitude toward reader and writer alike, and I love them.

Dianne Gardner, US: My art teacher once told me if you don't respect your work, no one else will either. It has been a dream of mine, ever since I began to write, to have my books in prominent bookstores and libraries. Just this last month, after five years of being self-published, I realized that dream.

A friend introduced me to the book buyer of Barnes & Noble in Silverdale, Washington. I had my first signing last month, and they've asked me back. The buyer there showed me all the shelves on which they are putting my books, plus they are making me a special label on the shelf with my name and "local author" tagged onto it. The store purchased a good quantity of every title I have on IngramSpark.

The buyer took me to his computer and showed me how well my novels have been selling and told me how happy he is with the result. I'm invited to sign books there anytime I want to.

He said that their store has such success with their local author program that other stores throughout Washington, and nationwide, are using the Silverdale branch as a role model for supporting local authors.

Because of the respect I've been given at both Barnes & Noble and IngramSpark, I feel validated as an author. I am selling books, not pages. Both companies are professional in their respect for my work, and I love the way things are going.

Jonathan Hope, UK: It was a surreal experience to be the featured author for an author event at Blackwell's bookshop in Oxford, England.

When I lived and studied in the city, Blackwell's was the place I'd go to buy books by my favourite writers and artists and,

Your Book in Bookstores

occasionally, to see them in person. It was here I heard Kazuo Ishiguro read from *The Unconsoled*, and persuaded Graham Swift to sign a well-thumbed copy of *Waterland*. ("At least I know this one's actually been read," he quipped.) The intercom announcement, "Ladies and gentlemen, please join us in five minutes in the Children's Department, where Jonathan Hope will be reading from his delightful new book, *A is for Donkeys*," made me feel as if I'd stepped through a mirror.

I don't have friends in high places, or a radical new promotional strategy to share. I simply walked into the shop, and asked.

Every book needs a spiel. When I began mine – "Hello, I'm the author of a self-published, quirky-stylish alphabet book...", the reaction of the chief buyer in the Children's Department wasn't hugely encouraging. Her words were polite enough, but her face said "I'm sending you packing as quickly as I can."

Then, miraculously, as she flicked through the book, her demeanour changed.

"Oh," she said, "but this is really LOVELY!"

The book's visual loveliness, I should explain, is not of my making. Italian illustrator Riccardo Guasco's retro-futurist style is the source of that.

Ricardo's images prompted me to create a traveling exhibition, something I would encourage any self-published writer of an illustrated book to consider.

The book launch in Bath was accompanied by a month-long display of prints at a local art space. Blackwell's liked the exhibition, and agreed to let me transfer it to their café.

Larry Garner, US: I have two books published independently and, although I had no trouble whatsoever displaying my books in independent, local bookstores in town, I had no luck with the big boys on the high street. Of course, my main target was the local airport bookstore, but getting in there seemed impossible. Twice I approached the owner of the bookstore. Twice I was politely told there wasn't sufficient shelf space. But I did have better luck with the manager. I approached her and said I would split the sales with her 50/50 while she was on duty. She agreed.

We have a rather large fly-in fly-out population (FIFO, mainly mining) in our location and, as both of my books are related to the mining industry, I targeted the flights most of the FIFOs took. I arrived a couple of hours before the flight and set up a small but very prominent stand in a corner of the shop, advertised the books as the "amusing tales of a FIFO miner," but pricing it was the winner: most books in the shop were priced between $24 and $29. I priced my books at $12.50.

I sold out!

I sold over a hundred books in two hours. Of course, the manager was the real winner; she took home over $600 for doing absolutely nothing. But don't think I wasn't happy.

Helena Halme, UK: I couldn't be an author without the constant support of an active independent shop, such as West End Lane Books. Just entering through the door, when that indescribable smell of (good) books hits you, you know you're among friends.

West End Lane Books is a small indie shop nestling in the arty, northwest London area of West Hampstead. The shop stocks a varied and interesting selection of books, and as well as hosting events with authors, they run two book clubs: West End Crooks, just for crime fiction, and a more traditional book club.

All clubbers get a 15% discount on the month's read. The @WELBooks Twitter feed is active and often hilarious.

West End Lane Books have supported my writing from the

very beginning, when I decided to go indie. They've stocked my first published novel, *The Englishman*, and also *Coffee and Vodka*, which made it into their "Staff Favorites" and keeps selling out. They also always have one or two signed copies of my books, which they hand-sell.

Katherine Hayton, New Zealand: I'm giving a shout-out to a bookstore in Upper Hutt, New Zealand. Named Writers Plot Readers Read (after a well-established writing group in the area named Writer's Plot), the bookstore is operating as a nonprofit determined to bring indie and self-published New Zealand writers into a bricks-and-mortar bookstore, often for the first time.

They have checks to ensure the writing is up to their quality standards, but otherwise every NZ indie author is welcome to stock there.

They feature a rotating writer-in-residence program, which means book buyers can get to meet and talk with some of the authors that they're purchasing, and they also run a lot of writer's workshops to help writers develop their craft. A writing desk is also able to be hired out in-store for a small fee if writers need somewhere to get away from their raucous daily life.

How's that for the perfect writing space, in the middle of a bookstore? Mmmmm. The smell of new books!

Karen Inglis, UK: I'm stocked by and have been supporting my local bookstores over the past few years, both the small independents and Waterstones in southwest London. They really do appreciate the support indie authors can bring through events and also helping point customers their way via social media and through fliers, etc. if holding events with them.

It had been on my to-do list for months to add a link to the "Find your local bookstore" sites in the UK and the US to my author site and my blog, and I finally got around to doing that.

I have always offered links to the bookstores local to me but offering links to the search pages of IndieBound is another way we can support our local and not-so-local bricks-and-mortar stores.

Jude Lennon, UK: I have used the following ways to get my books stocked in bookshops.

- Making contact with local indie bookshops via social media. Like their posts, comment on them then after a couple of weeks send a message and ask if you could pop in for a chat with your books. In every bookshop I've approached this way it's led to my book being stocked, a book event or some kind of collaboration.

- Just popping into local indie shops. We have the very supportive News From Nowhere store that welcomes walk-in authors. They do have guidelines as to the type of books they will stock (nothing religious).

- Holding book events in local bookshops. This is a great way to show support for the bookshop and have a chance to share your books. I've held a book launch or event for all of my books in Write Blend. I've also arranged book events with Kingsley & Co, a new children's bookshop (Frank Cottrell-Boyce was also on the Author Signing panel). Future events are in the offing with Tell Tales Books, another children's bookshop which is fairly local to me.

- I've also become a patron for Kingsley & Co. This bookshop is run as a charity and does lots of work giving the community access to literature. They have big plans for the future and hope to build on the success of their first Children's Literary Festival.

- I keep my eye out on social media for any bookshops who are actively looking for authors to get involved. I find Twitter hours and Facebook groups invaluable for this kind of information.

- I took advantage of WH Smith wanting to engage with more authors and bring people over the doorstep. It didn't result in huge sales for me but I've noticed this a lot. Picture books just don't seem to do as well at these kind of events as YA or adult fiction. I think this is because the pound shops are bursting with very cheap children's books. However, it was good for PR purposes.

- Getting involved in local literary events can also be a great way for bookshops to take note of your stock.

Regarding stores that aren't book specialists, I still find making links with local shops is a great way to find new stockists. A few local businesses stock my books and I give them shouts outs on social media especially during Just a Card Indie Week which is a week designed to encourage everyone to shop local and small.

Sue Miller of Team Author UK also arranged for an indie shop in Wirral to open a Team Author bookshop. There is a range of authors and genres available in the shop. I also held a book event for my first book for adults, a short story collection called *A Slice of Lennon*. The owner has turned the evening into a Christmas shopping night with 10% off everything else in the shop and provided mulled wine and winter Gin Slings.

Although we focus on getting books into indie bookshops, I always say it's about thinking outside the box, and I think other stores are a great market to crack and definitely more lucrative than the big retailers.

Chris Longmuir, Scotland: I approached my local branch of the UK bookstore chain Waterstones, in Dundee, but it was a different manager to now because this was way back in 2013. I traveled to Dundee with two copies of each of my books, and muttering under my breath that the worst that could happen would be a refusal. Quaking in my shoes, I delivered my spiel to the manager, showed him the books, and was amazed when he ordered twenty copies of each book. Needless to say I delivered them the next day.

Later that same year, Waterstone's launched my new book in the Dundee Crime Series, *Missing Believed Dead*, with an order of sixty copies of the book. The launch was a great success, and Waterstones ran out of chairs for those attending, so it was standing room only at the back. They continue to give me regular orders, and also launched my historical crime mystery, *The Death Game*, in 2014.

Apart from Waterstones, my books are stocked by my local book shop, Hoggs of Montrose, and I receive regular orders from Gardners, now the major distributor of books in the UK.

Mohanalakshmi Rajakumar, Qatar: When I first entered self-publishing I was learning about ebooks. Two years later, I was ready to launch a paperback. At the time, I didn't know the first thing about scheduling book events. I asked friends for recommendations of cafés that held events.

Christmas of 2012 we left our son with family to rush across town, wondering if anyone would even show up. They did. About twelve people, most of them friends who wanted to catch up.

"You don't know me, but I follow your blog," a bearded, spectacled man said, striding in with his daughter. An electric current ran through the rest of us. This is real, my husband's look said. Hope you have something good to say.

That same year, a few weeks later, we were staring at a "Closed" sign in Georgia, the supposed second stop of the book tour. The café had forgotten the New Year's Day event they had agreed to. We went to the movies instead.

I tried again six months later, as my new plan was to release all the ebooks as paperbacks, two a year. I wised up to independent bookstores and libraries, the living rooms of friends, and more or less anyone who wanted to talk to me about one of my books.

Some of them were great fun, like reunions, hugging old friends I hadn't seen in years, who kindly bought multiple copies of each title. Some of them were embarrassing, like the phone call I had to make while sitting alone at a signing table. "That's okay," I told the manager, who apologized for the fact no one said a word to me during my hour and a half vigil. (Except for the guy who chatted to me for ten minutes, ending with "I don't read books. Bye.") I didn't want to be a prima donna, since he had warned me volubly about low attendance before agreeing to host me. I drove away as quickly as I could.

In April, visiting Tampa for a conference, I began emailing bookstores, asking if anyone wanted to host me and my two paperbacks, the memory of that solitary event hovering in the shadows. "We don't do book events," came one gruff reply.

"Hi, this is Mohana. I sent you an email about doing a book event," I said to the person on the other end at the Old Tampa Book Company. I busied myself with my Twitter timeline to delay the sting of another brush-off.

"Yes, sorry, I've been so busy, but we would love to host you."

"You would?" I sat up straighter.

The conference I attended that month in Tampa had me scratching my head. "What am I doing here?" I thought, suppressing yawns at heavily academic presentations. That night I assembled myself for the event. And I was amazed by the wonderful people who showed up—strangers!—who hung on the edge of their seats and bought multiple copies of both my books. They had come in because of the strength of the shop's mailing list. "We did better sales on your night than we have all week," the shop owner said to me with a huge smile.

"Yes, thanks for being persistent," laughed the events person at a feminist bookstore in Atlanta. "We would love to have you."

Again in New York, strangers came into the volunteer-run shop, Bluestockings, to sit, listen, and ask questions about my work. They waited for me to sign copies for their friends and families.

In 2015 I did a five-stop book tour, in independent bookstores from New York to Atlanta. None of this would have happened without persistence and humility. (Not to mention writing new books.) If you have a story to tell, keep telling it. Keep asking—someone will definitely say yes.

Anna Sayburn Lane, England: "Great! I'd much rather buy it from a bookshop."

That was one friend's response when I told her she could buy my debut novel, *Unlawful Things*, from our local high street bookshop, as well as from Amazon.

I've always loved bookshops. From the days when I eagerly trotted up the road to spend my birthday book tokens as a child, I've thought of them as magical places, where nothing bad can happen and you might just find something wonderful.

So when I wrote my debut novel, I didn't dream of seeing my name on the Amazon Kindle best-seller list – I dreamed of seeing my book on display in my local bookshop, where anyone might pick it up while browsing, get engrossed and take it home.

But as a self-published author, could I make that happen?

Luckily I'd picked up ALLi's book ***How to Get your Self-published Book into Bookstores*** at the London Book Fair. It helped me prepare properly, understand what bookshops wanted, and make the best approach I could.

First one, then a second bookshop replied to say, yes please, they'd like to stock my book.

When I went in, I was glad I'd spent time working out how much I could afford to offer as a discount. One asked for a 60%

discount which would have left me out of pocket, but then accepted the deal I suggested when I held firm.

It helped to have the proposal in writing with me, so I didn't get flustered and agree to something I didn't want.

It also helped that I had a printed invoice with me (which I followed up with an emailed version), so they had my banking and contact details

The next couple of opportunities came by keeping an eye open.

A local newspaper interviewed me about the novel. In the same issue I read that another local bookshop had recently changed hands. I guessed that it would be worth approaching them – and as I hoped, they'd seen my interview and were keen to stock the book.

My biggest coup, however, was at Shakespeare's Globe, the theatre that is a recreation of the original Globe Theatre on London's South Bank.

Unlawful Things is a thriller about the fictional quest for a lost play by Elizabethan playwright Christopher Marlowe. One of the clues I'd made up was supposedly found in legal documents relating to the treason trial of Sir Walter Raleigh. I did a bit of a double-take when I walked past Shakespeare's Globe to see the winter season included not only Marlowe's most famous play *Doctor Faustus*, but also a recreation of the Raleigh treason trial!

I decided I had nothing to lose, so rang up and asked for the name of the shop manager, then sent her a copy of the novel, with a letter explaining the co-incidence, and the trusty AI sheet.

To my delight, she promptly replied asking for 10 copies of the book, which I delivered the next day.

While bookstore sales won't help me give up the day job just yet, it's been **a huge confidence boost** to see my novels on their shelves. Bookstores give a certain stamp of approval, so I've posted images of my book in bookshops on social media, tagging the relevant shop.

Bookstores are an important part of the whole book economy,

and all of us – readers and writers – would be poorer if they disappeared from the high street. Making the effort to understand what works for them, and encouraging readers to shop locally, benefits us all.

Margaret Skea, Scotland: My nearest bookshop, Mainstreet Trading in St Boswell's, which was Independent Bookshop of the Year for the UK not long ago, has an event space above the shop, and that's where I have my launches. I've found them very supportive.

They always hold stock of my books, but spine out in their very well-filled shelves. Someone needs to actually know they want them – they're hard to find by browsing – but when the booksellers were asked by HRH Prince Charles to be introduced to a local author, I was pleased they thought of me. He even asked me to sign his copy! It wouldn't have happened if I hadn't already made a working relationship with them.

There are still folk who don't want to shop online, and even it it's only a few copies at a time, it costs me nothing to have them stocked there, and I'm building a local profile, and that in turn leads to invitations to speak at events where I can sell more books.

And finally, the long-established British bookstore chain WH Smith welcomes self-published books, as illustrated by this case study of Richard VaughanDavies's event in his local branch.

Richard's historical novels were already being stocked by several local independent bookstores, which gave him the confidence to give WHS a try.

Your Book in Bookstores

Richard's moment-by-moment account of his event is useful for other indie authors who want to make the most of such opportunities in WHS and other bookstores. He also sets it into context as part of a much longer process in the author's career.

Richard Vaughan Davies, England: Sitting at a table with a stack of books in my local branch of WH Smith on a Saturday morning while the rain poured down. The staff were friendly and helpful, but it felt pretty lonely for the first half hour while my partner Barbara and I were setting up our stall.

Someone asked me where to find the newspapers, and another if we sold chocolate, but otherwise there was no interest in our table.

Deep gloom descended.

Then some kind friends called in, and a new customer started flicking through a copy. At the end of a brief conversation he actually bought one. We were off.

From then on we were meeting, talking, and even selling on and off for the rest of the day.

As a retired retailer this publishing route appealed to me. I am sure the cover sold it to them, and I doubt if the staff ever opened a copy, bless them. Anything to do with books was clearly a distraction from their main business of chocolates and cards but they were impressed that I had got the local paper interested, (they sent a photographer to the event too) and done an interview on a local online radio station.

Financially? We are not buying the house in Provence just yet. The profit margin on each copy sold was £1.23 (I gave Smiths a 40% discount off £8.99.) But we met a lot of nice people who gave me a clearer picture of my target reader.

And I learnt some **ground rules**:

- Smile and try to engage passing customers in some sort of chat.
- People will not willingly stop at your table unless they have come in specially.

- Be prepared to answer the same questions (about your book and nothing to do with your book) several times a day.
- Keep the atmosphere light. Make jokes. Have fun.
- Ask who they want the book signed for.
- Promote your next book.
- Use some display aids or props.
- Offer the shop books to display in the run-up to the event and afterwards

---

Debbie Young, England: Living 100 miles from my native London, I'd never have dreamed of trying to hold a London launch for *Best Murder in Show*, the first novel in my new Sophie Sayers Village Mysteries series, as I have no established contacts with any bookstores there. Then I came across an organization called Novel London, which runs a series of monthly reading events in various central London branches of Waterstones. Novel London's founder, Safeena Chaudhry, has a good relationship with the retail chain, and so by working in tandem with her, I was able to share a stage for a joint event with fellow ALLi crime writer JJ Marsh, who was launching her latest Beatrice Stubbs thriller, *Bad Apples*, compered by ALLi author Rohan Quine.

The store ordered twenty copies of my novel from IngramSpark, we had a packed house with standing room only, and we had our names and books promoted in-store and on the Waterstones website before the event, as well as on Novel London's.

I also got a professional-standard video for my own website as part of the deal. ALLi teamwork at its finest!

14

BOOKSTORES IN THE COMMUNITY
HOW WE ALL BENEFIT

Even if the preceding chapters have not convinced you to try to get your self-published books into bookstores, and you believe that your book will do better sold exclusively online or elsewhere, please do not turn your back on bookstores. They can still play a part in your success as an indie author and you can support bookstores in other ways.

This is not just altruism. We are independent authors, yes, but no author is an island. It benefits your author business long-term to have a robust, physical bookselling presence in our communities.

Bookstores, like libraries and schoolteachers, are ambassadors for the joy of reading—and all authors need readers. Unless these players keep shouting the message that reading is cool and fun, and an affordable source of joy and inspiration for all ages, our society risks forgetting the power of the written word. Binge viewing TV boxsets and the noise of social media will drown out the quieter joys of reading.

If bookstores continue to disappear from our shopping locations, individual authors and authors as a breed will be diminished. It helps us all if bookstores continue to present to shoppers of all ages the notion that buying books is A Good Thing. That instead of spending their disposable income on clothes or shoes or electronics or toiletries, they'll be better to invest in something fabulous to read? That rather than buy birthday and Christmas presents from random shops that they're unsure the recipients would like, a great book or a book token would be a better solution?

If we publish print books, visiting bookstores as customers increases our chances of getting our books stocked and and strengthens our relationship with the stockists who do carry our books.

Even if we don't publish print books, we should still patronise physical bookstores, and any non-specialist stores that sell books, even charity (thrift) stores. By spending time in bookstores, we recharge our creative batteries, stimulate writing and publishing ideas (eg the latest cover design or genre trends), and come away inspired and motivated.

So really, what's not to love about bricks-and-mortar bookstores? Next time you're out shopping, make sure you visit yours.

Ways to Support Bookstores

There are a lot of things you can do to support the bookstore without even leaving your desk.

Like their Facebook page, comment on their posts, share their posts. On Twitter, follow them, retweet their posts, #FF them for Follow Fridays. "Via their website, comment on their blog posts, follow their blog and subscribe to their online newsletter. "In every bookshop I've approached this way it's led to my book being stocked, a book event, or some kind of collaboration," says children's author Jude Lennon. Being a bookseller can feel like a thankless task sometimes, and strategic social media sharing can make their day—and probably earn some shares of your posts by return. If you blog, and host guests, consider doing an interview with your local bookstore proprietor or staff.

If you're a book blogger, consider also giving a shout-out to high street bookstores that you love, adding to them as you find more on your travels and on holiday.

Below are easy actions within your power to help bookstores survive, multiply, and thrive. Most of them will cost you little or nothing to carry out. Every time you do one, you'll be paying forward the love of reading.

- **Buy (indie) books!** If you plan to buy a book, and have a bricks-and-mortar store near you, buy it there. If the book you want is not in stock, the store can usually get it for you just as fast as any online ordering service. Asking for your favourite indie authors helps boost their reputation as well as sales.
- **Give books as gifts**—so easy to wrap and post at Christmas and birthdays.
- **Buy book tokens or bookstore vouchers**, a great way to encourage children and people of all ages to acquire the benefits of a reading habit. Yes, they might rather have an iTunes token, but book tokens have gone zonking up in the cool stakes with trendy plastic credit-card style designs. Didn't you love to receive book tokens when you were a kid? Pay that joy forward to the next generation, and you'll be helping a bookstore at the same time.
- **Add your bookstore stockist in the "buy" options on your author website.** To ensure they continue to be stocked, you need to drive a pull-through of demand: getting the books stocked is just the first part of the process. It will also score you a point with any local bookstore looking you up on Amazon—much better than if, when they visit your website, they find you're driving all your readers away from the high street to online retailers, like a Pied Piper of the book trade.
- **Remind people to support their local bookstore**, shop local, or however you prefer to word it. If their local bookstore (which in most cases won't be the same as yours) doesn't already stock your book, suggest they ask the proprietor to order your book for them. Your readers will be happy to receive that message, whether or not they choose to follow it. And if enough people start clamoring for your book in any particular shop, it's likely the proprietor will stock it for as long as the demand continues.

- **Visit your nearest bookstore** whenever you are on the high street or at the mall. Become a regular face there, befriend the staff, and before you know it, you'll find an opportunity to tell them about your book, even if you didn't have any intention of selling it there. Don't be shy of telling them about your book (or worse still, go in with a sense of entitlement)—most booksellers will consider authors premium-value customers, whether or not they stock your book, because they will perceive you as moving in circles where reading is king and having your own tribe of avid readers, to whom you're likely to recommend other books as well as your own. Most authors are also avid readers and book buyers. (If you're not, honestly, you should be.)
- **Support other authors' in-store events.** Whether or not you're interested in the author or their book, it's another way to become a familiar face and known supporter of the store. You'll also pick up tips on how to run an author event (or not!) and might even gain a new author friend to add to your own network.
- **Keep track of the events they hold there.** They'll have chosen them carefully to suit their clientele. See if you can dream up one of your own in a similar mold, either on your own or with indie author friends. Then go all out to bring an audience with you that buys books at the event, whether yours or others. Stage a successful event and you may even get asked back for more—because each time they see you in future, they'll have dollar/euro/pound signs in their eyes, seeing you as an asset to their business.
- **If you're staging local events elsewhere, show your support for the bookstore by inviting them.** Don't expect them to run a shop for you there, just ask them as your guest. Whether or not they wish to come, ask for a stack of their promotional fliers or bookmarks to give to your audience to promote their bookstore.
- **If your local bookstore runs a festival, as many do, offer your services as a volunteer.** Most festivals, small or large,

Your Book in Bookstores

rely on an army of volunteers to be financially viable. (*Opening Up To Indie Authors*, an ALLi campaign book, provides a useful reality check on the economics of festivals.) Volunteers tend to be either avid readers or aspiring authors. A great opportunity not only to score points with your bookstore but to network with potential readers and make new like-minded friends. Do it enough and the bookstore will start to see you as one of their ambassadors, which will make them more likely to be ambassadors for your book too.

- **Embrace bookish events.** If you're a children's or YA (young adult) author, for example, World Book Day provides a great opportunity to support your local bookstore by going in to be a resident author for the day, helping run activities for visiting children. World Book Night is the equivalent for adult readers.
- **Join their book group,** either offering to be a guest speaker to the book group, or join it as a reader.
- **If they have an in-store loyalty card, sign up for one.** You'll earn points or other benefits, and you'll also be helping them build greater knowledge of their local customers, Amazon style.
- **Ask if you could take a photo of the store to go on your website.** There's bound to be somewhere you can use it as an illustration, even if they don't stock your book. Then, when you use it, send them a link, which they may even share, or which might drive them to consider stocking your book in future.
- **Use their facilities.** No, I don't mean their the bathroom! If they have a coffee shop, and you plan to meet friends for coffee, or you want to eat out while you're shopping, use their coffee shop. If you enjoy writing in coffee shops, choose one in a bookshop. If you take part in a writers' group or book club, ask whether you can meet in the bookshop. When I refer to the local branch of a bookshop chain as my Bristol office, I'm only half joking. It's my city-center place of choice for meetings with other authors, and the chances of us both

leaving the shop without buying a book or stationery purchase are pretty slim. Consider buying a book as your notional rent for use of their space.
- **Show the booksellers simple kindness and good manners.** When buying a book, smile, chat (unless they're hugely busy), say something nice, and thank them for their help. My local bookstore proprietor makes no secret of the fact that he always welcomes gifts of coffee from the nearby bakery.
- **Treat staff like the professionals that you both are.** If you're seeking a book for a particular purpose, ask for and respect their advice. Their expertise never fails to amaze me, compared with the entertaining or horrifying recommendations from online algorithms.

Although we may be grateful to online retailers and distribution platforms for empowering the modern author, we can make room in our lives and businesses for retailers of all kinds.

Let's work together to keep bookstores on the high street as a universal temple to the author's trade, as embassies of reading, for the greater good of booksellers, writers, and readers all over the world.

The takeaway message from this chapter and book is very simple: ask not what bookstores can do for you—but what you can do for bookstores.

15

GOING FORWARD TOGETHER
JOINING THE ALLIANCE OF INDEPENDENT AUTHORS

At ALLi, we hope that this book, offered as part of our educational program, will unite and empower indie authors and bookstores alike to work long term for mutual benefit, together riding whatever other changes may arise in the business fo books.

This guidebook is just part of ALLi's continuing program to harmonize and synchronize the different worlds of author and bookseller. We also:

- share the latest headlines regarding the book trade in ALLi's Self-publishing Advice Center's weekly news roundup: SelfPublishingAdvice.org/news
- run informative posts in the Book Marketing section of the Self-publishing Advice Center blog, SelfPublishingAdvice.org.
- publish case studies of authors and bookstores working effectively together to inspire others to follow suit
- include events celebrating bookstores in our online calendar of global events of interest to authors

- encourage authors to support bookstores however they can, as listed in Chapter 12
- celebrate and highlight innovations that continue to make physical bookstores such special places, offering so much that is not available in the online retail environment
- wherever possible fly the flag for this philosophy.

At the same time, we have the greatest respect for authors who have decided not to pursue bookstores as a retail outlet. After all, as indie authors, that is our prerogative, and it is the combination of independence with mutual support that makes the world of self-publishing such an exciting and rewarding arena for us all.

If you're inspired by this book to take steps into selling via bookstores, do let us how you get on by commenting on the ALLi blog or emailing us through our contact form.

And if you'd like to continue the learning, we'd love to have you as an ALLi member. Even if you haven't published yet, you are welcome as an associate member. For more information on which type of membership would be right for you and about the many benefits of membership, visit ALLi's membership website at AllianceIndependentAuthors.org.

THE END

APPENDIX I: BOOKSTORES IN BOOKS

84 Charing Cross Road — Helene Hanff
The Bookseller of Kabul — Åsne Seierstad
Shadow of the Wind — Carlos Ruiz Zafon
The Bookshop Book — Jen Campbell
Books, Baguettes and Bedbugs — Jeremy Mercer
Weird Things Customers Say in Bookshops and (inevitably, because there must be an endless supply of material) *More Weird Things Customers Say in Bookshops* — Jen Campbell
The Yellow-Lighted Bookstore: A Memoir, A History — Lewis Buzbee
The Bookshop — Penelope Fitzgerald
You — Caroline Kepnes
The Diary of a Bookseller and <u>Confessions of a Bookseller</u> - Shaun Bythell

APPENDIX II: GLOSSARY OF SELF-PUBLISHING TERMS

#

100% black

Design term. The shade of black used in black and white printing. The CMYK color values for 100% black (also known as "flat black") are 0,0,0,100, which means it contains no colors other than black.

1/1

The book's interior will only be printed in black ink, with one "color" (black) on both sides of the page.

4/4

The book's interior will be printed in full color (4-color CMYK), with ink on both sides of the page.

4/0/0/4

Shorthand for how the cover will be printed, in the following order: front cover/inside front cover/inside back cover/back cover. Most books do not include printing on the inside covers, so they are 4/0/0/4, with 0 meaning no ink.

4-color black

see: **rich black**

99 Designs

Popular service offering crowdsourced book cover designs.
   see: **crowdsourcing**

A

abook

bbreviation of audiobook.
compare: **pbook, ebook**

acknowledgements

Recognition or honor given in a book to those people who have influenced the content or made a difference to the author.

ACOS (average cost of sale)

Accumulated total of all costs used to create a product or service, including overheads and fixed and variable costs.

acquisitions board

The people in corporate publishing who make decisions about what books to accept for publication.

ACX (Audiobook Creation Exchange)

Amazon-owned audiobook marketplace that matches authors with professional narrators and producers.

active income

Income derived from payment for hours worked. The defining feature of active income is that the income stops when work stops. Employee jobs and freelance work are examples of active income.
　　see: **passive income**

adhesive casebound

Standard binding for hardcover books, which uses glue to hold the interior text block to the cover.
　　also: **perfect binding**

advance

A sum of money paid to an author upfront by a publisher, on signature of a contract, as a prepayment of expected royalties issued in exchange for a license to publish. An author's advance is usually paid in four installments—on signing a contract, on delivery of the finished manuscript, on publication in hardback, and on publication in paperback and ebook. The advance needs to be "earned out" before the author receives more money.

advance information sheet (AIS)

A short document providing basic book details and information about a book's availability and ordering methods.
　　also: **sell sheet, fact sheet, pub sheet, book flyer**

advance print run

Printing of a book completed before the book's official release date, usually for publicity purposes.

advance review copy (ARC)

A draft of a book distributed to beta readers or reviewers prior to its publication.

compare: **proof**

Adobe InDesign

Popular professional book formatting and design software.

affiliate

To officially attach or connect to an organization.

affiliate marketing

A marketing arrangement popular with authors and self-publishing services by which an online retailer pays commission to an external website for traffic or sales generated from its referrals.

afterword

Closing remarks on the topic of the book or the process of writing the book. Can be written by someone other than the author.

aggregator

see: **ebook aggregator**

algorithm

A formula or procedure for solving a problem or carrying out a task. An algorithm is a set of rules and steps in a very specific order, such as a mathematical formula or the instructions in a computer program. Online book retailers, self-publishing services, and social media sites all use algorithms to calculate display of media and author and book rankings.

Anglo-American Cataloguing Rules (AACR)

A data content standard for describing bibliographic materials.

ALLi associate membership

Membership program for authors preparing their first book for self-publication. Also students of creative writing, multimedia, or publishing with an interest in author-publishing.

ALLi author membership

Membership program for authors who have published one or more books of 50,000+ words in length or equivalent, e.g. a number/series of shorter books, or children's books.

ALLi authorpreneur member

Membership program for authors earning their living from self-publishing and associated business. This membership is assessed—authors need to show evidence of 50,000 book sales in the past two years and/or KU or business equivalent.

ALLi organization member

Membership program for other author organizations who want to avail of ALLi's expertise in self-publishing.

ALLi partner member

Membership program for self-publishing services that agree to a code of standards and to being vetted for approval.

ALLi watchdog desk

ALLi service that monitors the practices of companies and individuals in the self-publishing services sector.

Amazon

American multinational conglomerate technology company that revolutionized publishing with the trio of e-reader, online retail store, and self-publishing technology for ebooks and audiobooks.
  see: **KDP, Kindle**

Amazon Author Central

A free Amazon service that allows authors to create author pages, promote their books, and monitor their sales ranking and reviews.

Amazon Marketing Services (AMS)

An Amazon program that allows sellers to bid on advertisements displayed alongside search results, product listings, and customer review pages.

Amazon Prime

A subscription service for Amazon customers that offers discounted shipping, access to free entertainment, and other benefits for authors, most notably the subscription reading service Kindle Unlimited.

Amazon Standard Identification Number (ASIN)

A unique ten-character identifier for an Amazon product.

Android

Mobile operating system designed primarily for touchscreen mobile devices such as smartphones and tablets. Developed by a consortium with the main contributor and commercial marketer being Google.
see: **Google, Microsoft**

app

see: **application**

appendix

Supplementary information that can follow a chapter or, far more commonly, at the end of a book, such as tables, source material, or statistics.

Apple Books

An e-reading, publishing, and retailing platform that makes books available for sale in 52 countries to be read on Apple Inc. devices like iPad and iPhone. One of the Big Five self-publishing technology companies,

Apple Inc.

American multinational technology **company** that designs, develops, and sells consumer electronics, **computer** software, and online services including the Apple Books e-reading and publishing platform.
also: **Amazon, Google, Microsoft**

application

A software program designed to accomplish a task for an end user (e.g. word processing or project management), as distinguished from the operating system that runs the computer itself.

application profile

Set of metadata elements, policies, and guidelines defined for a particular application or community.

ARC

see: **advance review copy**

artificial intelligence (AI)

Technology that replicates human behaviors and abilities conventionally seen as "intelligent." Used in publishing to underpin services like voice recognition, translation software, search, and sales engines.
 see: **voice recognition**

AskALLi

ALLi campaign that pledges to answer any self-publishing question that any individual or organization may have. Includes a podcast, email service, blog, and this book. See resources list for more.
 social media: #askalli

assisted publishing/assisted self-publishing

Umbrella term for all companies that provide personalized publishing services to authors for a fee. Some of these services bundle the seven processes of publishing into packages. Some offer hybrid publishing arrangements that adopt some of the practices of trade-publishing, including curation and physical bookstore distribution. Authors shopping in this sector need to exercise caution.
 includes: **hybrid publishing, partnership publishing, subsidized publishing**
 compare: **author-publishing, indie author**

Audible

An Amazon company that distributes audiobooks via a subscription model.

audiobook

A recording of a book being read aloud by the author or other narrator.
abbreviation: **abook**

author bio

A brief biography that may include a summary of books written, interests, and achievements.

author brand

A consistent message and representation of identity and image that helps readers to connect with authors and their books.
see: **book brand**

author collaboration

Authors formally working together, under a contract, to mutual benefit. Authors have always collaborated to write but author collaboration is a new and growing movement in publishing.
also: **joint venture**

author comps

see: **comparables**

author cooperative/collective

A group of authors who work together to leverage the skills of the group in order to advance members' publishing efforts.

author platform

A structure that gives leverage and visibility to an author and their books. An author platform gives the ability to sell books and allows the right readers, and others, to discover and understand what the author does and what to expect from their books. An author platform has three components: who the author is, what they say, and who they can reach.

autoresponder

An email service that sends an automatic response to incoming emails, which helps to reduce the amount of manual replies required.

authorpreneur

Entrepreneurial author–publisher who runs a successful business, by globally exploiting their own rights through a variety of formats and platforms.

author–publisher

An author who self-publishes for profit. May also publish other authors.
   also: **independent author, indie author, micro-publishers**

author-publishing

Another term for independent self-publishing by authors.

Author Solutions, Inc. (ASI)

A vanity press operating under a variety of imprints and that warrants caution.

B

Babelcube

Company that connects authors with translators and internationally distributes translated books.

back cover

see: **full cover**

backlist title

Trade-publishing term for a print book that has been published in the past but is still in print.

back matter

The sections of a book following the last chapter. Back matter can include an afterword, an appendix, a bibliography, a glossary, acknowledgments, an index.
  also: **end matter**

compare: **front matter**

back-of-the-room sales

Sales made by an author or publisher from a book table or booth at a live event. Widely used by nonfiction authors who are also speakers.

barcode

see: **EAN barcode**

Bertrams

The second-largest book wholesaler in the UK.
    bestseller rank
    see: **sales rank**

beta reader

A person who provides early feedback or a critique of a book prior to professional editing.

big data

An enormous supply of data, and often the analysis of such data.

bibliographic data

Specific information about a book including title, author, publication date, and price.
    see: **metadata**

Big Six: self-publishing

The six largest providers of self-published books, e-readers, and self-publishing production technology.

see: **Amazon, Apple, Ingram Spark, Google Play, Kobo, Nook**

Big Five: trade-publishing

The five largest, global traditional publishers: Hachette, HarperCollins, Macmillan, Penguin Random House, and Simon & Schuster. Formerly the "Big 6," until the merger of Penguin and Random House in 2013. Corporate publishing houses have been merging to preserve economies of scale.

BISAC

An acronym for Book Industry Standards and Communications, which is maintained and developed in the US by the Book Industry Study Group (BISG). Bookstores and libraries in the US may require publishers to provide a precategorization with BISAC when submitting data throughout the book supply chain.

BISAC codes

The BISAC subject headings list; a standard used to categorize books based on topical content.

bitcoin

The most popular cryptocurrency, generally deemed the first of its kind. The open source software comes with an elusive and mysterious history. Satoshi Nakamoto is the name used by the unknown person or persons who designed the bitcoin, but no one is really sure who made it. Now being used to buy books on blockchain.
  see: **blockchain**

BitTorrent

The most popular method of downloading files using a distributed peer-to-peer file sharing system. Controversial in publishing as some authors and publishers use the platform to spread their digital content throughout the internet and others see it as a threat to copyright.

bleed

Excess printed area that is trimmed after printing. Having bleed in your files ensures that full-page images take up the entire page and pages are not left with a fine white edge after trimming.

blockchain

Technology that facilitates a public, verified digital ledger and records transactions as a chain (string) of data, stored on a decentralized network. Information no longer needs intermediaries to facilitate trust as date, once entered, cannot be altered and is publicly verifiable. Blockchain enables smart contracts, digital assets records, and micropayment splits, all of which could benefit author-publishing.
    see: **Self-publishing 3.0 Campaign**

blog

A regularly updated section on a website; a useful way to help establish subject matter expertise and connect with readers.

blog hop

A list of web links that appears on multiple blogs, allowing readers to hop from one blog to the next in the series.
    also: **blog link-up**

blog tour

A series of pre-arranged blog posts, usually scheduled during the months just before and after a book launch.

blurb (1)

see: **book blurb**

blurb (2)

see: **endorsements**

Blurb (3)

Self-publishing service, particularly popular for illustrated books.

body copy

The text of the book that appears between the front and back matter.

Book2Look

A widget offering samples from a book alongside social links.

BookBaby

A popular self-publishing service that provides a wide range of services.

book block

PDF files that comprise all book content except the cover.
    also: **interior**

book blurb

Quote or paragraph of text on the back of a book, giving the reader a flavor of what the book is about, as well as information or quotes from other authors and celebrities, or media mentions.
    also: **cover copy**

compare: **book description, endorsements**

book brand

Identity and image of a book represented by the cover, copy, and blurb that indicate the book's promise to the reader.

see: **author brand, brand book**

BookBub

An ebook discovery service featuring a free daily email that notifies readers of discounted ebooks. Indie authors can submit their books for approval for deal offerings and advertise on the platform.

book categories

see: **BISAC**

book chainstores

Book outlets that share a brand and central management, usually with standardized business methods and practices, and spread nationwide or worldwide.

book comps

see: **comparables**

book description

Description of a book on online book retailers like Amazon, iBooks, and Kobo that enables readers to determine whether they want to buy a book. Typically longer and more targeted to purchase behavior than book blurb.

compare: **book blurb**

Book distribution

see: **distribution, aggregators, distributors, wholesalers**

book doctoring

see: **content editing**

Book Espresso machine

A machine that can print and bind any book as print-on-demand within five minutes.

book fair

A physical exhibition and convention for publishers, authors, and booksellers.

book marketing

Ongoing, repeatable activity which generates awareness of a book and its author among book distributors, retailers and readers.

compare: **book promotion**

book production

see: **production, publishing**

book promotion

Concentrated sales-driven activity behind a particular book for a particular period of time.

compare: **book marketing**

book review

Published opinion of a book. Book reviews appear in a variety of places and may be posted by professional reviewers or readers in a variety of outlets, including book review publications and retailer websites.
  see: **customer review, editorial review**

Books In Print

A catalogue, usually in digital format, primarily for use by bookstores and libraries, containing listings of millions of books with ISBNs; published by Bowker.

book trailer

A video advertisement for a book, much the same as a film trailer.

bound proof

Proof copy that looks like a finished "real" book, with cover attached and pages to final trim size. Used as ARCs.
  see: **advance review copy**

Bowker

A for-profit corporation that is the sole provider of and registrar for ISBNs in the US.

brand book

Official document explaining a brand's identity and presenting a particular brand's standards, visual identity, font, grammar and punctuation choices, etc.
  also: **brand guide, brand manual, style guide**

bricks-and-mortar (brick) bookstore

Used to distinguish a physical bookstore from online book retailers.

browsing

The process whereby a user of a system or website visually scans and maneuvers through navigation lists, results lists, hierarchical displays, or other content in order to make a selection, as contrasted to the user entering a search term in a search box.
see: **search, web browser**

business model

Replicable model for the successful operation of a business, identifying sources of revenue, intended customer base, products, and financing details. The ALLi posits ten possible business models for self-publishing authors, based on profit income.
see: **product mix, profit income, multiple income streams**

C

call to action (CTA)

The part of a marketing message that attempts to persuade a person to perform a desired action.

Calibre

ebook file creation and management software.

case bound

A type of binding and the industry term for a book in hardcover format. The cardboard cover can either be wrapped with printed paper (printed case wrap) or a solid material such as colored paper (which can be textured to look like linen) or leatherette. Solid color case wraps are typically foil stamped on the spine with the author's name and book title.

chainstore

Large company that owns many bookstores under the same name. The biggest chain in the US is Barnes & Nobles, and in the UK it is Waterstones.

CIEP Directory

Chartered Institute of Editing and Proofreading member directory of vetted editors, proofreaders and other editorial professionals. Freely searchable.

click-through

The process of clicking on a hyperlink or online advertisement to the target destination.

click-through open rate (CTOR)

Metrics used to measure the effectiveness of email marketing campaigns.

click-through rate (CTR)

The average number of click-throughs per hundred ad impressions, expressed as a percentage.

CMYK

A color model for print books, using cyan (C), magenta (M), yellow (Y), and black (K).
   see: **RGB, greyscale**

codex

The form of a physical book, which may be constructed of vellum, papyrus, or similar materials and handwritten, but most commonly now produced on paper and printed.

colophon (1)

Book production information, often including typeface details and information related to the artwork.

colophon (2)

The device or logo of the book's publisher or author.

commission (1)

A percentage of book sales paid to an author by a self-publishing service or retailer. Often confused with royalty payments.
    see: **profit income, royalties**

commission (2)

To order or authorize the production of publications, services, or materials.

comparables

Similar authors and their books.

comps

abbreviation: **comparables**

content editing

Editing with a focus on broad textual issues such as structure, pacing, character development, veracity, and relevance.

also: **structural editing, developmental editing, book doctoring, manuscript appraisal**

content editor

The person who conducts a content edit.

content marketing

The creation and sharing of useful material and media like videos, blogs, and social media posts to generate leads for a book or other author products or services.

conversion

The process of putting a manuscript into a digital format suitable for use by a publisher, such as converting a Word document into an EPUB file.

co-op advertising

Advertising whose cost is shared between or among different companies. In publishing this is when the publisher pays for print materials for customers, ads in the retailer's magazine, and store display, for example.

copyediting

Editing with a focus on the detail at the line level: syntax, grammar, verb tense, word usage, punctuation, and consistency. It is the copyeditor's job to ensure that the text, and any illustrative material, is expressed clearly and accurately. The copyeditor may also check basic facts such as dates, spellings of names, and arithmetic. In fiction, a copyeditor will look out for issues such as continuity and plot errors.

also: **line editing**

compare: **proofreading**

copyeditor

The person who conducts a copyedit of book copy (manuscript material).

copyright

The exclusive, legally secured right to reproduce and distribute works of original expression. Copyright is one of the main types of intellectual property and allows the copyright owner to protect against others copying or reproducing their work. Copyright affords an author the exclusive legal right to publish, perform, or record a literary work, to profit from it, and to authorize others to do the same. Works that fall outside of copyright are said to be in the public domain.

see: **publishing rights, piracy**

Copyright Bill of Rights for Authors

An ALLi campaign booklet that sets out eight fundamental rights that self-publishing authors need to be aware of in a globalized, digitized marketplace. Its aim is to ensure that copyright law remains robust and flexible enough to offer the incentive, protection, and reward it promises for authors who self-publish and license only some publishing rights to trade-publishers and other rights buyers. It aims to help self-publishers understand how to best avail of their economic and moral rights in today's rapidly changing digital publishing environment.

copyright page

The page traditionally in the front matter, but now sometimes found in back matter, that indicates the copyright status of a book. May also include cataloguing data.

CoreSource

Ingram Content Group's ebook distribution platform.

cost per click (CPC)

Internet advertising model used to direct traffic to websites, in which an advertiser pays a website owner when their advertisement is clicked. Also used to refer to the cost charged for each click-through from the ad to the product.
also: **pay per click**
compare: **cost per impression (CPI), cost per mille (CPM)**

cost per impression (CPI)

Also known as pay per impression. Internet advertising model, in which advertisers pay for the number of times an ad is shown on a website, regardless of whether or not it is clicked.
also: **pay per impression**
compare: **cost per click (CPC), cost per mille (CPM)**

Cost per mille (CPM)

1. An internet advertising model in which the advertiser pays each time the ad is displayed.
2. The cost to display an ad to 1,000 viewers.
compare: **cost per click (CPC), cost per impression (CPI)**

co-venture

Undertaking whose costs and responsibilities are shared by more than one company or publisher.
   see: **partnership publishing, joint venture**

cover design

Aesthetic layout on the covers of a book, usually intended to be attractive or alluring to the eye.

cover spread

The entire cover of a physical book, from the front, including the spine, to the back.

crawler

see: **web crawler**

CreateSpace

Now defunct Amazon-owned publisher and distributor of self-published print books. Replaced by KDP Print.
   see: **KDP, Kindle Direct Publishing**

Creative Commons

A nonprofit organization dedicated to building a globally accessible public commons of knowledge and "a more equitable, accessible, and innovative world culture" by helping people and organizations share knowledge and creativity more easily. Promotes the power of open licensing and global access.

Creative Commons license

A free, simple, and standardized way to grant copyright permissions, ensuring proper attribution while allowing others to copy, distribute, and make use of those works. An alternative to copyright notices that makes it easier for authors and others to share creative and academic work, as well as to access and build on the work of others.

creative self-publishing

An approach to author-publishing that emphasizes the unique qualities of an author and book in its particular marketplace. Creative self-publishing begins in the first (developmental editing) process of publishing and carries across all seven processes.
   see: **publishing**

credit line

Line of text that assigns credit to the owner of the copyright of the material it refers to.

crossover fiction

A young adult book that has potential for an adult readership, or vice versa.

crowdfunding

Funding a project by raising small donations from many contributors. Generally used in publishing as a step before a book is published. Many author–publishers run a crowdfunder as a preorder campaign for an upcoming title.
   see: **crowdsourcing**

crowdsourcing

Gathering information, feedback, or work on a project by requesting input from a large number of contributors. Crowdsourcing powers many digital publishing platforms, including crowdfunding platforms that raise money for book production or promotion. The book design and developmental editing processes can be crowdsourced, and publishers, including author–publishers, can use crowdsourcing to pitch ideas to readers, encourage reader feedback on a book, build a fan base, and incentivize readers to promote a book on social media.
  also: **crowdfunding**

cryptocurrency

Any digital currency, operating independently of a central bank, using encryption techniques to regulate the generation, verification, and transfer of funds. Using cryptography for regulation and security allows a decentralized system, meaning no central repository or administrator oversees the processes. Instead, it uses a blockchain. There are several kinds of cryptocurrency; three of the best known to date are bitcoin, ethereum, and ripple.

customer acquisition cost (CAC)

Measuring how much money a new customer has cost.
  also: **reader acquisition cost (RAC)**

customization

Modifying a book or other product or service using pre-established templates and scripts so that it fits a reader's unique preferences.
  see: **personalization, segmentation, targeting**

D

dashboard

n interface, usually web-based, that organizes and displays information on a single screen.

data (1)

Facts or numbers in a general sense.

data (2)

In computer science, information that exists in a form that may be used by a computer, excluding the program code.

database

A program used to store, query, and retrieve information.

dedication

Part of the front matter. Author's statement of appreciation or compliments to a specific person or group of people—or sometimes a place or thing.

demy octavo

A very popular book format, which measures 216 x 138mm.

design

The second process in the seven processes of publishing in which the book cover and interior text are configured. Book design consolidates the content, style, format, and sequence of the various components and elements of a book into a single coherent unit.

    see: **publishing**

developmental editing

    see: **content editing**

developmental editor

Person who deals with the overall organization of a manuscript rather than with detailed changes such as spelling and punctuation.

    also: **editorial, content editing**

digital printing

A method of mass-production printing using toners on a press that prints directly from a digital-based image. More suitable for shorter runs and most often used for print-on-demand books.

    compare: **offset printing**

digital rights management (DRM)

Systematic approach to copyright protection for digital media, including books. The purpose of DRM is to prevent unauthorized redistribution of digital media and restrict the ways consumers can copy content they have purchased. In practice in publishing, difficult to enforce and an irritation to readers.

see: **encryption**

digital signatures

A form of electronic authentication of a digital document. Digital signatures are created and verified using public key cryptography that ties the document being signed to the signer.

digital wallet

Any electronic device or application that allows electronic transactions, using cryptocurrency or government-based currencies.

direct-to-reader sales page

Page where readers can order books directly from the author, resulting in higher net profit.

discounts

There are two kinds of discounts in publishing: a retail discount, when books are offered at a reduced sale price to the reader; and a publisher's discount, offered to wholesalers, distributors, and retailers.

discoverability

The process of making a book visible and accessible to readers. In digital book publishing, the process of having good metadata, SEO,

and publicity, so books show at the top of relevant reader searches and are recommended by search engines.
see: **marketing, metadata, SEO**

disintermediation

The removal of intermediaries from a supply chain or transaction sequence. In self-publishing, the removal of agents, publishers, wholesalers, and others from writer-to-reader supply and transaction.

distribution

The fourth process in the seven processes of publishing, in which the book is made available to readers for purchase.
see: **distributors, wholesalers, retailers**

distributed ledger

A distributed ledger (also called shared ledger) is a consensus of replicated, shared, and synchronized digital data geographically spread across multiple sites, countries, or institutions where there is no central administrator or centralized data storage. Facilitated by blockchain technology.
see: **blockchain**

distributor

A company that works for publishers, supplying books to retailers (bricks-and-mortar or online), taking a fee and a percentage. May also provide other billable services.
compare: **ebook aggregator, wholesaler**

DOC, DOCX

Microsoft Word file types.

domain name

A registered alias for an IP address; the most basic URL of a website; e.g. selfpublishingadvice.org.

do not compete clause

Clause found in publishing contracts that bars author from publishing additional work that might compete with the book licensed to the publisher. Indie authors need to check the implications for such a clause on their self-published work.

download

see: **load**

DPI (dots per inch)

A measure of the resolution of a graphic file, a computer monitor, or potential printing density.

Draft2Digital

A popular ebook aggregator and publishing service.

dust jacket

A detachable outer cover that protects the book, printed with the cover design and wrapped around the case wrap, but not permanently attached. Usually for hardcover books.

E

EAN barcode

Barcode with the ISBN transferred into machine-readable form. The electronic scanning lines printed on the back cover or book jacket are encoded with information about the book, such as the title, publisher, and price.

see: **ISBN**

ebook

Abbreviation of electronic book. Can be read on dedicated readers or on devices like phones, tablets, or computers.

ebook aggregator

An ebook distribution service that circulates ebooks to a number of retailers and other distributors, e.g. Draft2Digital, PublishDrive, StreetLib.

compare: **distributor, wholesaler**

economy of scale

Savings in per-unit cost achieved by mass production.

editorial

The first process in the seven processes of publishing, in which the words and subject matter of a manuscript are revised, amended, improved, and rearranged for clarity, simplicity, brevity, and artistic effect.

see: **publishing**

editorial review

A professional critic's opinion of a book published online or in a periodical.

also: **review**

e-ID/electronic identity

Identity in a digital format. Often involves an identity card with embedded chip, certification, and separate signatures for authentication and verification. e-ID is legally binding and used to sign smart contracts in a number of countries.

email marketing

The promotion of products or services to list subscribers via email.

embossing

Special treatment used to raise a portion of a book cover, often the title. Can only be applied to paperback books or dust jackets.

encryption

Encoding mechanism used to prevent unauthorized users from reading digital information and also for user and document authentication. Only designated users or recipients have the capability to decode encrypted materials. Encryption is vital to fintech, the blockchain, and anything else that needs to be secure. Data, like names and numbers, is turned into a code using algorithms (mathematical formulas). A key is required to turn that code back into useful data.

see: **digital rights management**

encumber

To create restrictions on how publishing rights may be used.

endorsements

Short reviews of a book written by a well-known author, professional, or personality in a genre/niche. Endorsements can be placed on the front or back cover, or in the introductory pages of the book, and used for promotional purposes.

compare: **blurb**

end matter

see: **back matter**

endsheet

Paper glued to the inside of a hardcover case, which also becomes the first (unprinted) interior page of the book. Standard endsheets are white, but they can be colored or printed.

endorsement quotes

Short reviews of a book written by a well-known author, professional, or personality in the author's niche.

epilogue

A section or chapter at the end of a book that comments on or draws conclusions about what has happened or been explained within the text.

EPUB

A common ebook file format.

e-publishing

The publication of digital works such as ebooks.

e-reader

A handheld device on which electronic versions of books, newspapers, magazines, etc. can be read.

e-tailer

An online retailer.

ether

The native cryptocurrency of the Ethereum platform, used to pay for computational services there.

Ethereum

A blockchain-based cryptocurrency platform that runs smart contracts, already in use by writers and artists.

Ethical Author

ALLi campaign.
 see: **Ethical Self-Publishing**

Ethical Self-Publishing

ALLi campaign encouraging and educating about best practices in self-publishing. Includes a code of standards for indie authors and self-publishing services, showing their support for the principle of putting readers first. Authors display a website badge "I am an ethical author" and services agree to being vetted by the ALLi watchdog desk.

exclusivity

A publishing contract that binds an author solely to one self-publishing service, trade publisher, or retailer.
 compare: **go wide**

F

Facebook

The largest online social media and social networking service, allowing users, who sign up for free profiles, to connect with friends, work colleagues, customers, or people they don't know. This is the flagship brand service of the namesake company, which also owns Instagram, WhatsApp, Oculus VR, and many other apps, brands, and services.

Facebook advertising

Advertising via Facebook that allows a choice of target audience based on demographics, behavior, or contact information.

fintech

Financial technology that is allowing the disruption of traditional financial networks, facilitating innovation and the possibility of an author-centric financial model.

first rights

The exclusive right to publish a work for the first time.

Fiverr

Budget marketplace of freelancers offering digital services in 250+ categories.

fixed web design

Outmoded website design where images and text always remain the same size, rendering it unreadable on some devices.

font

A specific typeface of a certain size and style.
compare: **typeface**

footnotes

Reference citations and supplementary information at the bottom of a page.

foreword

An introduction to a book, usually written by someone other than the author.

format

The size, type, and binding of a book; e.g. ebook, paperback, hardback, large print.

formatting

The process of designing a book for electronic distribution, with the desired layout, fonts, and appearance.
compare: **typesetting**

formatting tag

Written tag inserted into a manuscript to alert a formatter.

forum

An online place where people with common interests or backgrounds come together to find and share information and discuss topics of interest.

front list

Traditional term for books in their first year of publication.

front list title

A book published recently, usually in the current year.

front matter

The sections of a book preceding the first chapter. Can include acknowledgments, copyright page, contents page, dedication, foreword, preface, and other publishing information. Since the advent of digital publishing, much of this information has been moved to the back of the book, to maximize the benefit of "Look Inside" functions on Amazon and other retailers.
  also: **prelims**
  compare: **back matter**

full cover

Single image file containing a back cover, front cover, and spine.
also: **back cover**

full-service distribution

Wholesalers and distributors who perform a broad range of services, such as stocking inventories, operating warehouses, supplying credit, and employing salespeople, as well as delivering goods.

G

galley copy

see: **proof**

genre

A general category for a creative work, such as romance, science fiction, mystery. The three macro genres are fiction, nonfiction, and poetry. Within these there are other large genre categories (e.g. children's books) and subgenre categories (e.g. children's books aged 4 to 7). Knowing a genre, subgenre, and niche is essential for effective book marketing.

see: **niche**

ghostwriting

Writing all or part of a book on behalf of a collaborator whose name will be listed as the author.

glindex

Combined book glossary and index.

go direct

To publish books to a retailer without the use of an intermediary service like an aggregator or distributor.

Goodreads

A social media site owned by Amazon, which is just for books. Readers connect with friends, get book recommendations, write reviews, and make reading lists.

Goodreads advertising

Pay-per-click advertising on Goodreads.

Goodreads giveaway

An online book giveaway that any Goodreads member can enter.

Google

American multinational technology company that specializes in internet-related services and products, including online advertising technologies, a search engine, cloud computing, software, and hardware products, all used extensively by self-publishing authors.

Google Adwords

Text-based ads that show up next to Google search results, graphic display ads that show up on websites or apps, or YouTube video ads that show up during videos.

Google Play

Digital distribution service for books and other content, operated and developed by Google. One of the "Big Six" self-publishing platforms.

Google Play Books

Google Play Books Partner Center is where authors and publishers submit their books, so that readers can search for and preview these books on Google Books and, in a growing number of countries, buy the ebook on Google Play.

Google Preview

Google Play's interface for viewing excerpts of an ebook before purchase.
compare: **Look Inside the Book**

go wide

To publish or sell books through a variety of services and retailers.
compare: **exclusivity**

greyscale

A color model that uses only shades of black.
see: **CMYK, RGB**

guest blogging

Writing a post or short article for someone else's blog.

H

halftone

A method of representing an image with dots of varying sizes.

hardback/hardcover

A book with a hard cover, rather than a paper cover; or the cover itself.

hard return

Pressing the enter or return key to force a line break instead of allowing the text to flow naturally.

hashtag

A word or phrase immediately preceded by the # symbol. When you click a hashtag, you see other social media updates containing the same keyword or topic.

headshot

A professional-looking head-and-shoulders photograph used for promotional purposes.

hit

Accessing a web page or a file, image, or script on the page.

house ad

A self-promotional ad run on an author's own website to sell their own products.

HTML

Abbreviation for hypertext markup language, a standardized system for tagging text files to achieve font, color, graphic, and hyperlink effects on website pages.
compare: **XHTML, XML**

hybrid author

A term sometimes used to describe an author who uses both trade-publishing and self-publishing services.
compare: **hybrid publishing, indie author**

hybrid publisher/hybrid publishing

A hybrid publisher provides a mix of trade-publishing and self-publishing services in the same contract. Hybrid publishers have very varied business models, methods of working with writers, and approaches to marketing and distribution but all curate the books they help to publish. Many also offer physical bookstore distribution. Although there are ethical and reputable hybrid publishers, there are many more substandard services that have turned to a hybrid publishing model, sometimes as a means of camouflaging exploitative vanity press operations.

compare: **hybrid author, vanity service**

I

iBooks

Former trade name for Apple Books.

impression

A single display of an advertisement or web page.

imprint

A name used by a publisher to identify their books. A single publishing entity may have multiple imprints, which are usually genre-specific.
    see: **publishing houses**

inbound marketing

Marketing model that relies on the initiative of customers to find, connect with, and purchase a product, rather than advertising benefits;

e.g. content marketing, social media marketing, search engine optimization.

income streams

Different methods of earning income. Examples include **earned income**, derived from trading time for money; **business income** derived from accumulating assets; and **royalty income** derived from licensing a product or idea.

see: **active income, business models, passive income, product mix, royalties**

independent ("indie") bookseller

Retail shop, not owned by an individual, partnership, or small business, selling books to the general reader.

see: **book chainstores**

independent ("indie") publisher

Smaller publisher outside of the "Big Five" publishing corporations. Ranging in size from medium enterprises to micro-publishers like individual companies and self-publishing authors.

see: **author-publishing, micro-publisher**

independent ("indie") self-publishing services

Companies and freelancers hired by independent, self-publishing "indie" authors who upload their own books directly to self-publishing distributors and operate as the creative director of their book publishing and author business. Services in this sector vary from individual local freelancers to huge, global companies like Amazon KDP and Apple Books.

InDesign

see: **Adobe InDesign**

index

Quick-reference list found at the back of many nonfiction works, directing readers to specific subject matter in a book and allowing readers to easily find particular information.

indie author

An author who acts as the creative director of their own books, whether through self-publishing, assisted self-publishing, or traditional publishing.
   compare: **self-publishing, traditional publishing**

Indie Author Rights Program

ALLi program that educates and encourages authors to selectively license publishing rights to trade-publishers at home and overseas, TV and film producers, and other rights buyers.

infrastructure as a service (IaaS)

Instant computing infrastructure, provisioned and managed over the internet; e.g. Amazon Web Services (AWS), Google Compute Engine (GCE).

Indiegogo

Popular crowdfunding platform for authors.

Ingram Content Group

American company that manufactures and distributes print-on-demand books. A division of Ingram Industries.
  see: **IngramSpark, Lightning Source**

Ingram ipage

An online books search, order, and account management platform for bookstores.
  see: **CoreSource**

IngramSpark

A large producer and distributor of print-on-demand books and ebooks.

initial coin offering (ICO)

An unregulated means of crowdfunding by which money is raised for a new cryptocurrency, selling tokens in the currency to raise money.

Instafreebie

A streamlined way to send book copies to reviewers, beta readers, or bloggers by providing a link for people to download a book for free.

institutional sales

Book sales to schools, libraries, and universities, especially by children's book and textbook publishers.

intellectual property (IP)

Thanks to copyright law, books are protected as intellectual property, a bit like a trademark or patent. Intellectual property rights are the

protections granted to the creators of intellectual property (including authors) by the law.
   see: **Copyright Bill of Rights**

interior

All content within a book, except the covers.
   compare: **book block**

internet search engine

see: **search engine**

iPad

Proprietary tablet computer device designed and marketed by Apple, used to read ebooks and consume other digital content. Runs the iOS operating system.

IPR License

Platform for authors, publishers, and agents to list and license publishing rights, providing access to a global marketplace. Owned by Frankfurt Book Fair with the Copyright Clearance Center.

ISBN (international standard book number)

A unique numeric identifier for a particular edition and format of a book. Each version of the book (e.g. paperback, hardback, ebook) will have a different ISBN. The owner of the ISBN is the publisher of record.

J

jacket

Publisher term for a book's front cover. The key internal publishing meeting where decisions are made about a book's cover is called "jackets."
also: **dust jacket**

joint venture (JV)

A business arrangement in which two or more parties agree to pool their resources for the purpose of accomplishing a specific task. This can be a new project or any other business activity.
see: **partnership publishing, author collaboration**

JPEG

A format for compressing image files; the most common image format used by digital cameras.

Jutoh

ebook formatting software compatible with Mac, Windows, and Linux.

K

KDP

See: **Kindle Direct Publishing**

key phrase

see: **keyword**

KENP

see: **Kindle Edition Normalized Pages**

keyword

Any significant word or phrase in the title, subject headings, or text associated with an information object.

Kickstarter

Popular crowdfunding platform for authors.

Kindle

Proprietary ebook reading devices designed and marketed by Amazon. Enable users to browse, buy, download, and read ebooks and other digital content via wireless networking to the Kindle Store.

Kindle App

Application providing access to Kindle books right in a web browser, phone, or other device. The app syncs the furthest page read, bookmarks, notes, and highlights between Android, PC, Mac, iPad, and any Kindle device, including Audible audiobooks.
   see: **Whispersync**

Kindle Cloud reader

Web-based version of Kindle that enables the reading of Kindle books on a web browser without a Kindle device and also enables offline reading when not connected to the internet.

Kindle Direct Publishing (KDP)

Publishing and distribution platform for ebooks provided by Amazon to authors and publishers.

Kindle Edition Normalized Page Count (KENPC)

Amazon KDP payment method for books enrolled in KU and KOLL, calculated using standard formatting settings of font, line height, and spacing and measuring the number of pages read in a book, starting at the start reading location (SRL). Non-text elements within books including images, charts, and graphs count toward a book's KENPC.

KDP Select

An optional KDP program that requires exclusivity in exchange for promotional tools and subscription.
see: **Kindle Unlimited (KU), Kindle Owners' Lending Library (KOLL)**

Kindleboards

A popular online discussion forum dedicated to publishing on Amazon.

Kindle Owners' Lending Library (KOLL)

KDP program that allows Amazon Prime subscribers to read one free ebook per month. Enrolment in KOLL is mandatory for KDP Select authors.
see: **Kindle Unlimited (KU)**

Kindle Scout

An Amazon program in which readers nominate books for publication under the Kindle Press imprint.

Kindle Singles

Amazon's digital, curated imprint for short works, primarily novellas, short fiction, and long-form journalism.

Kindle Store

ebook retail store operated by Amazon as part of its online retail website that can be accessed from any Kindle reader or Kindle mobile app.

Kindle Unlimited (KU)

KDP program that allows subscribers to read ebooks in the KU catalogue for free. Enrolment in KU is mandatory for KDP Select authors.

see: **Kindle Owners' Lending Library (KOLL)**

Kindle Worlds

Amazon's digital publishing platform for fan fiction.

Kobo

A Toronto-based Canadian company that sells ebooks, audiobooks, e-readers, and tablet computers. The name Kobo is an anagram of book.

Kobo Writing Life

Digital self-publishing platform that allows authors and publishers to easily create, edit, and upload ebooks to Kobo.

L

lamination

Thin coating of plastic over a book cover. Can be gloss (more hardwearing) or matte.

landscape

Term used to describe the orientation of a book, where the book is wider than it is tall.

compare: **portrait**

launch party

Celebration of the publication of a book. Can be hosted at any location, but popular spots include bookstores, libraries, coffee shops, or the author's home. A virtual book launch can also be hosted online. Launches are less significant for digital publishing (ebook and audiobook) than print sales in bookstores, though a lot of activity in early weeks can establish a book's ranking in online stores.

LCCN (Library of Congress control number)

A unique identifier assigned to books by the US Library of Congress.

lead magnet

A specific deliverable (like a free ebook download or other product) used to entice readers to join an email list.

legacy publishing

A somewhat derogatory term for trade-publishing.

license

Legal permission granted to someone other than the original holder of a right; e.g. permitting a publisher to print a work for which someone else holds the copyright.
compare: **copyright**

limited edition

A book printed in limited numbers, usually for special editions.

line editing

see: **copyediting**

Lightning Source

Ingram printer and distributer of print-on-demand books, mainly used by the trade-publishing sector.

Linux

Operating system that powers Android.

list

The books a publisher or imprint has available for purchase or has commissioned.

list price

The recommended retail price of a book as set by the author or publisher.
   also: **recommended retail price, retail price**

literary agent

Person who acts as an intermediary for an author in transactions with trade-publishers and other rights buyers, in return for a percentage of an author's advance, royalty income, and sometimes sales commissions. Literary agents can also manage an author's career or business, from helping to develop book ideas to negotiating book deals with publishers and other rights buyers. Some agents also facilitate the relationship between author and editor.
   see: **rights licensing**

litho printing (lithography)

A method of mass-production printing using wet ink and printing plates. More suitable for longer print runs.
   also: **offset printing**
   compare: **digital printing**

load

The process of moving or transferring files or software from one disk, computer, or server to another. To *upload* means to transfer from a local computer to a remote computer; to *download* means to transfer from a remote computer to a local one.

Look Inside

An Amazon feature that allows customers to view excerpts from an ebook or print book before buying.
    see: **Search Inside**
    compare: **Google Preview**

M

Mac

omputer hardware developed by Apple Inc. for its Macintosh systems, with original focus on the graphical user interface.

MacOS

Apple-Macintosh operating systems

makeready stage

Point in the printing process when a publication is ready to be printed.

manuscript

Text and images of a book prior to the interior layout process. Electronic text file prepared by the author for editors and designers.

manuscript appraisal

see: **content editing**

manuscript conversion

see: **conversion**

marketing

The fifth process in the seven processes of publishing, which generates awareness of a book and its author among book distributors, retailers, and readers. Marketing is ongoing, repeatable activity that positions an author and their books to be discoverable.
   see: **discoverability, promotion, publishing**

marketing plan

Strategic plan that details the documents, activities, and deliverables needed to market an author and their books.

mass-market paperback

Smaller, less expensive version of a book that is usually printed well after the hardcover and trade paperback versions have been made available.

media kit

A package of key information to send to media or journalists, retailers, book bloggers, event planners, editors, or anyone who plans on writing about an author and their book. May include an author photo and bio, a book cover image, a full synopsis, a one-sentence description, book details, frequently asked questions, an excerpt, and reviews or media coverage.
   also: **press kit**

media list

A collection of media outlets and contacts to reach out to in order to increase awareness of a book.

media outlet

Any channel for disseminating news about a book, such as newspapers, magazines, radio shows, TV shows, online news sites, podcasts, or blogs.

metadata

Bibliographic information about a book including title, author's name, book description, ISBN, publisher, genre category, publication date, and price. This automatically feeds into various data systems, including publishing catalogues and stock lists, and is passed on to the rest of the trade including customers. Includes data to optimize discoverability in online search, including keywords—words that someone may type into search engines when looking for a book.
  see: **bibliographic data, categories, keywords**

metadata mining

The automated extraction of metadata from electronic documents.

micropayments

Financial transactions of very small sums of money.

micro-publishers

Small publishing enterprises, including sole trader author-publishing authors. Some micro-publishers provide specialized information by subscription to a niche readership.

micro-publishing

Publishing performed by micro-publishers. Also publishing involving very small print runs or individual volumes printed on demand.

Microsoft

American multinational technology company that develops, manufactures, licenses, supports, and sells computer software, consumer electronics, personal computers, and related services. Makes its software services such as Office and Outlook available on all devices, including its own Windows system.

Microsoft Publisher

Desktop publishing software from Microsoft with emphasis on page layout and design. Not widely used by self-publishers as it does not convert to EPUB.

Microsoft Windows

Operating system developed and marketed by Microsoft.

Microsoft Word

Word processing software

MOBI

Amazon's digital format for Kindle ebooks.

N

NaNoWriMo

Stands for National Novel Writing Month. A nonprofit program that encourages novelists all over the globe to write a 50,000-word novel in 30 days. NaNoWriMo is both the event and the name of the nonprofit organization that coordinates the event each year.

NaPoWriMo

NaNoWriMo spinoff: National Poetry Writing Month. Like NaNoWriMo, it is an international event.

natural language processing (NLP)

Subfield of linguistics, computer science, information engineering, and artificial intelligence concerned with the interactions between computers and human (natural) languages, in particular how to program computers to process and analyze large amounts of natural language data to produce works like books.

see: **artificial intelligence**

NCX

Navigation control file for XML applications, used in EPUB documents to define the table of contents.
see: **TOC**

Netgalley

An online book reviewing site. Book reviewers, librarians, booksellers, educators, and media professionals request complimentary ebooks in exchange for reviews.

networking

Using and expanding a social network or sphere of influence to promote a book.

newswire distribution

Circulation of news through a service intended for journalists and media outlets.

niche

A specialized target market characterized by a particular interest, topic, or subject.
see: **genre**

Nielsen

The sole registrar for ISBNs in the UK and Ireland.

nonexclusive contract

Legal agreement in which the publisher does not exercise exclusive rights over the materials published in a book.

Nook

Barnes & Noble's line of e-readers and its associated retailer.

novel

Long-form fiction, more than 50,000 words in length.
compare: **novella, short story**

novella

Mid-form piece of fiction from 10,000 to 50,000 words.
compare: **novel, short story**

O

offset printing

A method of mass-production printing in which the images on metal plates are transferred (offset) onto rubber blankets or rollers and thereby to paper.

compare: **digital printing**

off-thebook attention

Marketing term referring to mention made of a book outside the context of a book review, such as plugging a book on a talk show.

online bookseller/retailer

Internet-based bookstore.

online marketing

Using online methods to advertise, promote, and sell books and other products.

Open Up To Indie Authors (OUTIA) Campaign

ALLi campaign encouraging bookstores, libraries, reviewing bodies, literary events, and prizes to find ways to include self-publishing writers in their programs, events, festivals, prizes, listings, and reviews. The campaign includes an email network, a petition, and a guidebook for organizers and events.

social media: #PublishingOpenUp

operating system

Software that manages the hardware resources of a computer or device. Acts as a mediator between the user and the computing system. A software program runs a computer, as distinguished from an app (application), which is installed into an operating system in order to enable users to perform specific tasks.

abbreviation: **OS**

see: **application, Mac, Microsoft Windows, Linux**

OS

Abbreviation of **operating system**.

out of print (OP)

When a distributor has no copies of a print book on hand and future reprints are unplanned or unknown.

out of stock

When the distributor temporarily has no copies of a specific title on hand.

P

P2P lending

P2P means peer-to-peer, or person-to-person, and refers to anything that is decentralized and direct. P2P lending is loaning money to individuals without the systems and processes typically put in place by traditional financial institutions. Instead, the transactions are often handled by digital platforms that use an algorithm to manage transactions between parties.

PageRank™

A proprietary link-analysis algorithm developed by Google to assign a numerical score to each document in a set of hypertext documents based on the number of referring links. The algorithm also takes into account the rank of the referring page; thus a link from a high-ranking page counts more than a link from a low-ranking page.
see: **algorithm**

Pages

Formerly iPages. Apple Inc.'s word processor marketed as an easy-to-use application that allows users to quickly create documents on Apple devices.

paperback

A book bound in stiff paper or flexible card.
  see: **mass-market paperback, trade paperback**

paper weight

Not the actual weight of the sheet of paper but its thickness and sturdiness; e.g. everyday paper used in most home printers is 20lb (20#) paper weight.

partnership publishing

A publishing arrangement in which the author and the publisher both contribute financially to the book's production, sharing risks and rewards. Sometimes referred to as hybrid publishing and sometimes used as a euphemism for vanity publishing.
  also: **shared publishing, subsidized publishing**
  compare: **author collaboration, hybrid publishing, joint venture**

passive income

Income not directly tied to active work. Typical passive income sources are front-loaded with low-paid or unpaid active work, while the bulk of the income comes later. Interest, dividends, and royalties are prime examples of passive income.

pay per click

see: **cost per click**

pay per impression

see: **cost per impression**

pbook

A physical, printed book generally constructed of a number of sheets of paper, bound in cardboard.
   see: **codex**

PDF (portable document format)

A file format popular for its cross-compatibility, particularly in keeping layout and fonts as intended. The preferred file format for print-on-demand and fixed layout ebooks.

pen name

A fictitious name, adopted by an author and printed on the title page and by-line of their works in place of their real name. Self-publishers often use different pen names for books they write in different genres.
   also: **literary double,** ***nom de plume*****, pseudonym**

perfect bound

Standard binding for paperback books that uses glue to hold the text block to the cover.
   see: **adhesive casebound**

permafree

A book permanently available for free from online retailers; a strategy used to increase visibility and gain new readers by giving away a book, often the first in a series. Also used by affiliate marketers or associated product promoters.

permission

Agreement from a copyright holder that permits the reproduction or publication of copyrighted material. Also the process of securing agreements from a copyright holder.

permissioned blockchain

Blockchain with access restricted to a particular group.

personalization

The ability to insert a reader's own content and personal data (e.g. children's names), which intensify the reading experience and supports reader empowerment and agency.
   see: **customization, segmentation, targeting**

PickFu

A service that helps authors carry out split tests on cover designs and book titles.

piracy

Individuals or companies that copy and distribute books for free or for profit, without obtaining permission from the author or publisher. Piracy is an infringement of copyright. In recent years there has been a growth in ebook piracy websites. There is debate about how much piracy actually costs authors and publishers in lost sales, and some authors have even welcomed piracy as a discoverability tool.

pitch emails

Emails targeting publicity contacts and other influencers to get coverage for a book or author.

plant costs

Initial costs incurred by a traditional printer in preparation for the first printing run of a given title.

platform

The computer hardware or online system used to run a program or digital tool.

platform as a service (PaaS)

Provides a computing **platform** that typically includes operating system, programming language execution environment, database, web server, etc.; e.g. AWS Elastic Beanstalk, Google App Engine, Windows Azure.

plot

Flow or succession of actions in a story.

POD

see: **print-on-demand**

podcast

Online audio broadcast available on a website or as a download.
 see: **ALLi podcast**

portrait

Term used to describe the orientation of a book, where the book is taller than it is wide. Most books are portrait.
 compare: **landscape**

preface

Introductory section of a book, usually written by the author. May contain information on why the book was written or how to use the book.

prelims

see: **front matter**
 compare: **back matter**

premades

Pre-made book cover design.

preorder

A marketing tactic used by authors to offer readers the opportunity of reserving a copy of a book prior to its official release date.

press-ready files

Generally, two PDF documents of a laid-out interior and full cover.

press release

An official announcement that provides information about an event to reporters, bloggers, and other media outlets, including publication date and endorsements.

Prime Reading

A program that allows Amazon Prime subscribers to read free ebooks from a catalogue of approximately 1,000 titles selected by Amazon.

print-on-demand (POD)

Printing books in small quantities, as needed and to order, using digital printing methods.

print ready

Used to describe the final layout file of a book, usually in PDF format, that is ready to go to the printer.

print run

The number of copies printed in a single order.

printing signatures

In offset printing, interior pages are printed on large sheets of paper that are then folded into a group, called a "signature," typically in groups of 16 or 32. Minimum signature size is 4 pages. For books with a page count that cannot be easily divided, additional blank pages are used to complete printing signatures.

production

The third process in the seven processes of publishing, in which the book is constructed, in audio, electronic, or print format.
see: **publishing**

product mix

The total range of products and services offered by an independent author.
see: **business models, multiple income streams**

profit income

Profit income is derived by selling a product (e.g. a book) for a higher price than it costs to make. Profit income is the main source of income for self-publishing authors, the amount left over after the costs of the seven processes of publishing a book, or the costs of producing another product, project or service, have been covered.
see: **business models, royalties, commissions**

promotion

The sixth process in the seven processes of publishing, being concentrated sales-driven activity behind a particular book for a particular period of time. Promotion takes one book and brings it to its target readers, with enticement to buy.
see: **marketing, publishing**

proof

A copy of a book printed for final inspection and correction of errors. Publishers also use proofs to get people excited about a book in advance of publication, and they are sent to journalists and bloggers to review, as well as to retailers. Proofs can be very simple with blank covers but closer to publication look more like the finished book.

also: **galley copy**
compare: **advance review copy (ARC)**

proofreading

The final editorial stage after the book is formatted and typeset, to pick up remaining essential text errors and check the layout: e.g. misspellings/typos, accuracy of captions, headings, page numbers.

Pseudonym

see: **pen name**

public domain

Books outside of copyright protection are said to be in the public domain, which means anyone may reproduce, sell, or otherwise use any part of them, without having to obtain permission.

publication date (pub date)

Official date when a book is released to the public for sale. In bookstore distribution of print books, pub date is set for some days after the book's arrival in stores to synch with marketing and publicity.

publicist

Professional or press agent who promotes a book, often by generating free advertising.

publicity tour

Public circuit an author makes to publicize a book, either prior to or soon after the publication date.

publishing

The procedure that turns an author's manuscript into a book to be sold and/or licensed at a profit. Publishing comprises seven processes: editorial, design, production, distribution, marketing, promotion, and rights licensing.
compare: **book production**

publishing house

Corporate publishers are made up of smaller companies that operate independently called "houses"; e.g. Penguin Random House is made up of nine publishing houses. Each house is in turn made up of several publishing imprints.
see: **imprints**

publishing rights

The right to exploit an author's intellectual property by publishing a book, or producing associated publications and formats, e.g. TV show, film, and translation. Self-publishing authors retain all rights, aside from those selectively licensed to publishers and other rights buyers in a particular marketplace or format. Publishing rights are generally granted to a rights buyer by license, in return for a royalty (i.e. percentage of sales income). Flat-fee payment offers for publishing rights should generally be rejected.
see: **subsidiary rights**

PubMatch

Rights management platform that allows authors and publishers to trade publishing rights and permissions with publishers, agents, and other rights buyers. Owned by the London Book Fair.
purchasing recency, frequency, and monetary
see: **RFM**

Q

QR code

Quick response code. A machine-readable code that consists of black and white squares and is typically used for storing URLs. Essentially a variation of a barcode, QR codes are now readable by smartphones and publishers use them to draw readers from print content to an online purchase page, supplementary digital content, or social media pages.

Query letter/email

A one-page communication sent to influencers, literary agents, publishers, and other rights buyers, in an effort to get them excited about a book or other project proposal.

R

Reader acquisition cost (RAC)

easuring how much money a new reader has cost to acquire.
also: **customer acquisition cost (CAC)**

recency

see: **RFM**

Reedsy.com

Online marketplace for indie authors to hire vetted designers, editors, and marketers with proven publishing experience.
see: **CIEP Directory of Editors**

region

A geographical area served by a publisher or retailer. For example, Amazon operates separate regional websites for the US, Canada,

Mexico, the UK, India, France, Germany, China, Japan, Italy, Spain, the Netherlands, Australia, and Brazil. Publishers and other rights buyers may license rights in specific territories.
 also: **territory**

remainder

A book returned to the publisher after not having sold, often offered for later sale at a discounted price.

residuals

Royalties paid to a writer for a repeat of a play or television show.

responsive web design

Web design that resizes a website to fit any screen on any device: desktop, mobile, or tablet. All author websites should be responsive as increasing numbers of people read ebooks on phones and other small devices.
 compare: **fixed web design**

returns

Books returned from book retailers to the publisher and refunded after failing to sell.

reversion

The process of reclaiming rights licensed to a publisher.

reversion of rights clause

Clause found in many publishing contracts that outlines the conditions under which rights will revert to the author.

review

see: **book review**

RFM

Digital book marketing principle standing for purchasing recency, frequency, and monetary. **Recency** asks, how recently did the reader purchase? **Frequency** asks, how often does the reader purchase? **Monetary** asks, how much has the reader spent? High RFM means high ranking on online store algorithms.

RGB

A color model for digital and online use, using red, green, and blue.
   see: **CMYK, greyscale**

rich black

Range of deeper black hues made up of all four colors of ink and sometimes called 4-color black. Should be used for large areas of black in books printed in color.
   see: **100% black**

right readers

The specific readers that are most likely to buy a book, based on demographic information and areas of interest.

rights

see: **publishing rights, subsidiary rights**

rights licensing

Assigning the right to publish, produce, or otherwise exploit a book's content or characters in exchange for royalties (a percentage of sales revenue), or (less often, and less desirable) a flat fee.

see: **selective rights licensing**

ROI

abbreviation: **return on investment**

The amount earned from a book, product, or project versus the amount of money it cost (fixed costs and associated costs) to produce.

royalties

Payment in return for the right to license a copyright, usually expressed as a percentage of the book price. The main source of author income in trade-publishing. Often confused with sales commissions paid by self-publishing services.

see: **profit income, commissions**

S

SaaS

ee: **software as a service**

saddlestitch binding

Pages are bound in the gutter with two staples around which the book folds. Used for booklets.

sales funnel

A process that converts a website and social media visitors into paying readers by convincing them to purchase books.

sales handle

A one-sentence call to purchase found on the back of a book and in its advertising.

sales rank

A ranking calculated by Amazon on the basis of daily sales and downloads of a book.
also: **bestseller rank**

sans-serif font

A font without serifs. Popular sans-serif fonts include Helvetica, Arial, and Avenir.
compare: **serif font**

Scrivener

Popular editing and organizational software designed specifically for self-publishing authors.

search engine

Software program that collects data taken from the content of files available on the web and puts them in an index or database that web users can search in a variety of ways. The search results provide links back to the pages matching the user's search in their original location.

Search Inside

see: **Look Inside**

secondary rights

The right to resell a work after its first publication.

segmentation

A marketing strategy that breaks a target market and breaks it into smaller groups based on their interests, common needs, or priorities.

see: **customization, personalization, targeting**

selective rights licensing

Assigning the right to publish, produce, or otherwise exploit a book's content or characters on a nonexclusive basis, carefully limiting format, territory, and term.
see: **rights licensing**

SelfPubCon

Online author conference run twice yearly, in association with ALLi.

self-publishing

A form of publishing in which the author oversees the publishing process, retains control over creative decisions and disposition of publishing rights, and bears the costs of production.

self-publishing 3.0 (1: concept)

The concept of self-publishing 3.0 is that digital technology gives any author (who has acquired the necessary writing and publishing skills) the means to increase their income through building a sustainable and scalable author business.

Self-Publishing 3.0 (2: Campaign)

ALLi's Self-Publishing 3.0 campaign aims to raise the average income for authors and poets through enterprise education and author empowerment. The campaign lobbies the literary and creative industries in seven global territories and advocates for a truly independent self-publishing sector.

The Self-Publishing Advice Center

Popular outreach service from ALLi offering a blog, podcast, books, ratings charts, and other resources. SelfPublishingAdvice.org

The Self-Publishing Advice Podcast

Advice and author interview podcast from ALLi, broadcasting twice weekly.

self-publishing service

A company or freelancer commissioned by an author to provide any of the seven processes involved in publishing a book: editorial, design, production, distribution, marketing, promotion, or rights service. Some companies offer full-service and multi-service packages.

compare: **assisted publishing, hybrid publishing, partnership publishing**

sell sheet

see: **advance information sheet**

SEO (search engine optimization)

The process of making a web page more easily findable and indexed by search engines; or more relevant to particular topics in order to attract more visitors.

serialization

A subsidiary publishing right by which extracts from a book may be published by a newspaper or magazine.

serif font

Font with a small line attached to the end of each stroke. Popular serif fonts include Garamond, Baskerville, Minion Pro, and Times New Roman.

service marks

Trademarks used to identify services are usually called service marks.
 see: **trademarks**

shared publishing

Another term for partnership or hybrid publishing.

shelf life

The time an unsold book remains on the shelf of a retail store before being replaced by fresh or better-selling stock.

short discount

Smaller-than-typical discount on books purchased by retailers and wholesalers.

short-run print

Printing of a limited number of copies of a book in a single print run. Can now be as low as 300–400 copies. For fewer copies, digital printing is generally a better option.

short story

Short-form piece of fiction under 10,000 words.
 compare: **novel, novella**

Shutterstock

Popular crowdsourced provider of high-quality licensed images, videos, and music.

side-sewn

Special binding method used for hardcover books with low page counts (fewer than 64 pages). Printing signatures (see below) are stacked on top of one another and then sewn together as one before being glued into the hardcover case. Side-sewn bindings require special file preparation for books with crossover images.

see: **printing signatures**

slush pile

Derogatory term for the unread, unsolicited manuscripts submitted by authors to traditional publishers for consideration.

small press

Smaller publishing house that releases books often intended for specialized audiences.

smart contracts

Computer programs that automatically execute legally binding contracts. These automated and often blockchain-based computer protocols facilitate, verify, or enforce digital agreements, saving time and reducing costs in common legal and financial transactions and potentially replacing lawyers and banks.

Smashwords

A popular ebook retailer and aggregator.

Smyth-sewn

A special binding method used for hardcover books. Each printing signature is sewn individually before all signatures are sewn together and then glued into the hardcover case. This binding affords maximum durability.

see: **printing signature**

social media

Websites and applications that enable users to create, publish, and share content and participate in online networking. One of the main methods by which authors connect with potential readers.

social media handle

The name, always preceded by @, that is used on various social media platforms including Instagram and Twitter.

social media marketing

Use of social media platforms to connect with customers to build a brand, increase sales, and drive website traffic. Social media vary in popularity across time but some major platforms that have held popularity for more than a decade are Facebook, Instagram, Twitter, LinkedIn, Pinterest, and YouTube. All of these are used effectively by authors to build readership and drive sales.

software as a service (SaaS)

One of the three main categories of cloud computing, SaaS is a method of software delivery and licensing in which software is accessed online via a subscription, rather than being bought and installed on individual computers. The software is licensed on a subscription basis and is centrally hosted; e.g. Asana, Convertkit, Dropbox, Google Apps, Slack, ZenDesk.

also: **on-demand software, software plus services**
compare: **infrastructure as a service (IaaS), platform as a service (PaaS)**

spam

Unsolicited email, often with product information or a sales pitch.

speaker recognition

see: **voice recognition**

special sales

Book sales through non-bookstore outlets such as restaurants, gift stores, and health spas.

spine

The edge of the book's binding. The spine connects the front and back covers and faces outward on a bookshelf.

spine width

Calculation for the width of a book's spine in the cover file, based on the page count, including any additional blank pages needed to complete printing signatures, and on the weight of the paper stock used.

spiral bound

A method of binding in which wire or plastic is wound through holes punched along the side of a book.

split A/B test

Comparing two versions of something to see which performs better (sometimes called split testing).

start reading location (SRL)

Amazon KDP term that identifies the location where a book begins, used for determining pages read under the KENPC payment method. Set generally at the first page of chapter one.
   see: **KENPC**

structural edit

see: **developmental editing**

style (1)

Author's personal way of writing, which can include word choices, punctuation preferences, and formatting choices.

style (2)

Specific layout of a text, or a variation of the presentation of a word (such as page headers or the use of a specific font).

style guide

Detailed listing of an author's preferences in spelling usages, character names, grammar, dialogue, and punctuation idiosyncrasies. Many authors develop these on their own and send them to their editors as a guide, but an editor may create one during the copyediting process. Many editors use a generally accepted guide for the book's genre, e.g. *The Chicago Manual of Style*.
   also: **style sheet**

subscript

A character (number, letter, or symbol) that is set slightly below the normal line of type. It is usually smaller than the rest of the text.

subsidiary rights

In a publishing contract, the rights that are kept separate from the core publishing license between publisher and author and governed by other (sublicensing) arrangements. They include the right to publish a work based on the original material but in a different format; e.g. serialization rights in newspapers or magazines, translation rights, film or TV rights, merchandising rights, or print rights in a different country (territorial rights). Digital publishing has seen rights that were traditionally subsidiary become core, most notably audiobook rights.

Self-publishers generally retain digital rights and selectively license subrights, limiting the format, term, and territory as much as possible.

also: **subrights**
see: **publishing rights**

subsidized publishing

Another term for publishing services offered to authors by companies on a fee-based or hybrid publishing model.

see: **assisted publishing, partnership publishing, hybrid publishing**

superscript

A character (number, letter, or symbol) that is set slightly above the normal line of type. It is usually smaller than the rest of the text.

subtitle

Subordinate title of a book giving additional information about its content. Most typically used in nonfiction to demonstrate value.

swipe copy

Copy-and-paste text that can be used by others for ease. Widely used in affiliate marketing to make promoting an offer more convenient for affiliates.

synopsis

Overview of what the book is about and what makes it special. A synopsis will be sent to editors, publicists, sales teams, retailers, journalists, reviewers, and others. A synopsis should be longer than the cover blurb and should include a tantalizing summary of theme, structure, or plot, a hint of the conclusion (fiction and nonfiction) and style (literary work and poetry), and the most noteworthy features of the book and/or author.

T

table of contents

A list, usually in the front matter, of the book's chapters or main sections and their opening page numbers.

tagline

A catchphrase or slogan, especially as used in advertising. Typically used in fiction to attract potential readers to the story concept.

target audience, target market

see: **right readers, targeting**

targeting

Devising a promotional campaign to appeal to a segment of readers based on their particular genre, niche, or interests.

see: **customization, personalization, segmentation**

template

Document that includes a default set of objects like headings, fonts, and images, used as a starting point when creating other documents. Useful when similar publications have to be frequently created.

term

A fixed period applying to a publishing or rights purchase contract. The rights buyer seeks to extend the term, the rights seller to limit it.

terms and conditions

The stipulated or agreed requirements or conditions under which an action is undertaken or agreement reached; e.g. the amount of an advance, the percentage discount awarded by a publisher to a bookseller, the sales commission charged by a self-publishing platform.

termination clause

Section in a contractual agreement that specifies particular behavior, actions, or events that would result in nullification of the contract.

territory

see: **region**

thumbnail

A small representation of a larger image, intended as a preview.

TOC

see: **table of contents**

token

A type of security issued in digital form. For example, a READ token gives the owner the right to read an ebook.

Track Changes

Feature of Microsoft Word and Apple Pages that allows authors and editors to collaborate on a manuscript while giving the opportunity to accept or reject each other's alterations.

trade bookseller

Any company that distributes books to the general public, including superstores, chain stores, independent booksellers, and online retailers.

trade paperback

A book bound with a paper or heavy stock cover, usually with a larger trim size than that of a mass-market paperback.

trade (traditional) publisher

A company that invests in publishing a manuscript, submitted to them by an author, and controls most creative and marketing decisions. Trade publishers bear the cost of production and promotion in exchange for a sizable percentage (typically 90%+) of the receipts from a book.

trademark

A type of intellectual property consisting of a recognizable sign, design, or expression that identifies products or services of a particular source from those of others. These badges of origin can take many forms; e.g. words, slogans, logos, shapes, colors, and even sounds. Trademarks can be registered.

see: **service marks**

traditional distribution

Where books are printed ahead of time and stored at a warehouse from whence book wholesalers and distributors fulfill orders.

trim size

The dimensions of a print book, specifically the page size, expressed always as width first, then height.

Tweeps

Users of the social media platform Twitter.

typeface

A set of letters, numbers, and characters that are all in the same style and that are used in printing.
  compare: **font**

typesetting

Professional preparation of a book for print with the desired layout, fonts, and appearance. *compare:* **formatting**

U

Ulysses

Popular "distraction free" writing software targeted at authors who want to focus on the content of their words.

unbound proof

Proof with interior pages not bound together, which means pages may not be trimmed to the final book size, and the color and quality of the ink may also be different.

unit cost

The production or base cost of printing and putting together a book.

unique visitor (unique)

An individual who accesses a website.
  compare: **hit**

universal link

A link that simplifies the process of author discoverability by directing book customers to one link that allows them to choose their preferred online retailer.

university press

Publishing house owned and operated by a university. Such presses typically issue academic material, often including works by their own academics.

unsolicited manuscript

Manuscript sent by an author to a publisher who did not request it. Most publishers say they do not read unsolicited submissions.

Unsplash

Popular crowdsourced provider of free imagery and pictures.

upload

see: **load**

Upwork

An online marketplace connecting businesses and skilled professionals.

URL (uniform resource locator)

The address of a web page.

UX

What a user of a particular product (e.g. ebook, e-reader, author website) experiences when using that product.

V

vanity publishing (press)

Traditionally, any publishing service that charged a fee. Now the term for an exploitative service that trades on authors' dreams of publication, with excessively high fees, substandard service, and often the pretense that they are trade-publishing houses.

compare: **partnership publishing, assisted publishing, hybrid publishing**

virtual book tour (VBT)

Advertisement strategy centered on publicizing a book on the internet, including ads on websites that the target audience frequents and book giveaways.

vlog

A blog that contains video content. This growing segment of the blogosphere is sometimes referred to as the vlogosphere.

voice recognition

The ability of a machine or program to receive and interpret human voice dictation, or to understand and carry out spoken commands. Voice recognition has gained prominence and increased use with the rise of AI and intelligent assistants, such as Amazon's Alexa, Apple's Siri, and Microsoft's Cortana.

W

watchdog

Person or group monitoring the practices of companies providing a particular service or in a particular sector.

see: **ALLi watchdog desk**

Whispersync

Amazon's technology that syncs furthest page read, bookmarks, notes, and highlights between any Kindle app or reader and Android, PC, Mac, iPad, and other devices using the Kindle app. Also allows a reader to switch back and forth between a Kindle ebook and Audible audiobook.

web browser

Software application that enables users to view and interact with information and media files on the web. Mozilla Firefox, Google Chrome, and Apple Safari are examples of web browsers.

see: **browser**

web crawler

Software program that systematically traverses the web, either for the purpose of generating a searchable index of web content or to gather statistics.

website

Collection of related electronic pages (web pages), generally formatted in HTML and found at a single address where the server computer is identified by a given host name.

wiki

Collaborative website that contains pages that any authorized user can edit. Wikis typically retain all former versions of each page, allowing the revision history of a page to be tracked and for unwanted revisions to be reversed.

Wikipedia

A free, collaborative, volunteer-driven, web-based encyclopedia that utilizes wiki software to allow anyone to edit articles. en.wikipedia.org/wiki/

Windows

see: **Microsoft Windows**

wholesaler

A company that works for bookstores, libraries, and other book outlets. They buy books in large quantities from publishers at high discounts and sell them to bookstores and libraries at a mid-level discount.
    see: **distributor**

word of mouth

Publicity through recommendations from friends, family, and associates. The most effective form of book promotion.

Word

see: **Microsoft Word**

World Wide Web

Vast, distributed wide-area client-server architecture for retrieving hypermedia documents over the internet.

World Wide Web Consortium (W3C)

Main international standards organization for the World Wide Web.

X

XHTML

bbreviation for extensible hypertext markup language, a hybrid of HTML and XML.
compare: **html, xml**

x-height

The height of a lower-case x, considered characteristic of a given typeface or script.

XML

A computer meta-language that allows users to define their own customized markup languages, especially in order to display documents on the internet.
compare: **html**

Y

YA

Young adult fiction.

YouTube

A free video-sharing website that makes it easy to watch online videos. Authors can create and upload their own videos to share with others.

Z

zero rating

British and Commonwealth tax term denoting goods or services that are taxable for VAT (value added tax), but with a tax rate of zero.

INDEX

A
acknowledgments 79, **163**
Aer.io 116
aggregators *see* ebook aggregators
AI (advance information) sheets 87–9, 127, **164**
airport bookstores 24, 27, 89, 134
Alexander, Piers 25–7
Allen, Brooke 46–7
Alliance of Independent Authors (ALLi) *iii–iv*, 13, 14, 18, 153–4, **166–7**
Amazon **167**
collection points 37
"currently unavailable" listing 83
effect on bookstores 16, 17
in physical bookstore market 7–8
pricing policy 36
subscription reading services 3
vendor accounts 116
see also KDP; KDP Print

American Booksellers Association 37–8, 39
Apple Books 21, **168**
approaches to booksellers
chain bookstores 56, 80, 138
examples of good practice 87–9, 136–7, 141
how not to do it 60–3
step-by-step guide 95–101
targeting local bookstores 56–7, 80, 96
see also AI (advance information) sheets
art exhibitions 133
Association of Publishers for Special Sales (APSS) 55–6
audiobooks 2–3, 4, **170**
Australia, book industry 33, 35
author events 52, 103–10, 111, 121, 150
experiences of 132–4, 136–7, 138–40, 143–5
author websites 89, 104, 116–17, 136, 149, 151

B
Barnes & Noble 9, 35, 38–9, 46–7, 132
Bartons Bookshop, Leatherhead, UK 40
Bates, Matt 27
Batten, Prue 131
Beaton, MC 59
Blackheath Bookshop, UK 9, 48
Blackwell's, Oxford, UK 132–3
Blanchard, Jill 63
blogs 136, 148, **176**
Bluestockings, New York, US 140
book clubs 135, 151
book festivals 93, 137, 150–1
book launches 103–10, 138
see also author events
book presentation *see* cover design; production standards
book readings 109–10
book tokens 149

book tours 139, 140
Books and Ink Bookshop, Winchcombe, UK 100
"Books Are My Bag" campaign 39
booksellers 10–11, 33, 42–3, 49
see also approaches to booksellers
Booksellers Association 39, 40
bookshop.org 53
bookstore proprietors 11, 49
bookstores
importance of 147–8
reasons for selling through 25–8
trading context
discounts 24, 119–20, 121, 122–5, 141
future environment 42
health of market *iv–v*, 15–17, 37–9
impact of online retailers 16, 17, 35–7
just-in-time delivery 41
past environment 30–3
payment terms 129
present environment 33–41
sale or return 40, 66–7, 69, 125–8, 128–9
special orders 72–3, 121–2
stock acquisition 65, 67–8
successful bookstores 64–5
ways to support 18, 63–4, 136–7, 147–52
see also airport bookstores; chain bookstores; independent bookstores; indie-only bookstores; local bookstores; nonbookstore outlets; specialist bookstores; unusual bookstores
Borders 46, 47
Bottomley, Nic 17, 35, 38, 40, 67, 68, 99
Boyce, Lucienne, *To The Fair Land* 30–1
Bromley, Andy 33, 71–2, 84, 86, 92, 103, 117, 122
Buzbee, Lewis, *The Yellow-Lighted Bookshop* 30

C

Campbell, Jen, *The Bookshop Book* 49, 89
Capri, Diane 87
Castle, Di 63
centralized purchasing 56, 80
chain bookstores 8–9, 45–8, 56, 67–8, 80
see also Waterstones
Chapters 35
Charles, HRH The Prince of Wales 142
Chaudhry, Safeena 145
children's books 25, 79, 133, 137, 151
Clays 92
CLC Bookstore, Dundee, UK 106
coffee shops, use of 151
color printing 84–5
consignment (litho) printing 91–3
consignment deals 103, 111
Corbett, Hereward 68, 72, 78
Cottrell-Boyce, Frank 137
cover design 27, 76–7, 78–9, **189**
COVID-19 pandemic *iv–v*
Curran, Connor 9
Cutler, Robin 22–3, 69

D
Daunt, James 8–9, 39, 80
Davis, Jane 91–2
Deal Bookshop, UK 9, 48
discounts **195**
bookstore 24, 119–20, 121, 122–5, 141
distributor and wholesaler 85–6, 122, 123, 124–5
distribution
supplying direct 116–17, 128–9
through distributors 68–72, 83–6, 90–3, 117, 122–5, **195**
see also IngramSpark; KDP Print; Lightning Source
Doppler, John 22, 53

Draft2Digital 21
Dymocks 35, 131

E
ebook aggregators 21–2, **199**
ebooks 4, 16, 21–2, **199**
Edmonds, Hattie Holden 129
Emporium, Cromarty, UK 106
Espresso Book Machine 3–4
Etsy.com 116–17

F
Facebook 63, 137, 148, **205**
fixed/minimum pricing 31–2, 33
forewords 79
Foyle, Christina 32–3
Foyles 9, 13, 32–3, 47, 126
France, book pricing 33
front cover *see* cover design
full-service distribution 68, 69–70, **208**

G
Gardner, Dianne 132
Gardners 26, 71, 92–3
Garner, Larry 134
"going wide" 21–2, **211**
grocery superstore chains 32, 34
Guasco, Riccardo 133

H
Halme, Helena 134–5
Harpenden Books, UK 9, 48
Harry Potter series 5
Hatchards 47
Hawkesbury Press 81

Hayton, Katherine 135
Hewett, Helene 39
Hoggs of Montrose, UK 138
Holloway, Dan 77, 109–10
Hope, Jonathan 132–3
Howey, Hugh 59, 112
Hunter, Andy 53
Hutchison, Barry 63–4

I
illustrations, display of 133
imprints 81–2, **217**
independent bookstores 8–9, 14–15, 38, 48–9, **218**
India, discounts 123
IndieBound 39, 136
indie-only bookstores 9, 51–3
Inglis, Karen 136
Ingram *see* Aer.io; IngramSpark; ipage
IngramSpark (IS) 24, 41, 66, 69, 70, 71, 83–4, 85–7, 91, 124, 127, **220**
in-store book printing 3–4
in-store events *see* author events
ipage 71–2, 124–5, **220**
ISBNs 24, 82–3, 84, **221**

J
Jefferson, Patti Brassard 52
Jones, Wendy 105–6
Jud, Brian 55
Just a Card Indie Week 137

K
Kala, Ritesh 72, 123
KDP (Kindle Direct Publishing) 21, **226–8**
KDP Print (KDPP) 24, 41, 69, 82, 83–4, 85, 86–7
Kingsley & Co, Bootle, UK 137

Kobo 3, 21, **228**

L
Lane, Allen 31
Larsson, Bjorn 117
Lennon, Jude 136–7, 148
Lewis, Tim 97
libraries 104, 121
Lightning Source 69, 85, 91, 124, **230**
LinkedIn 97
literary events 137
litho printing 91–3, **231**
local bookstores 56–7, 80, 96, 136, 147–52
Longmuir, Chris 126, 138

M
Mainstreet Trading, St Boswell's, UK 142
Marsh, JJ 145
Matador 70
metadata 69, 83–4, **235**
Miller, Sue 137
Minett, Rosalind 127
minimum/fixed pricing 31–2, 33
Morton, Alison 90, 108
multi-author events 109–10
see also author events
Myers, Karen 54

N
New and Secondhand Books, Swanage, UK 63
News From Nowhere, Liverpool, UK 136
Nicholls, David 33
nonbookstore outlets 10, 54–6, 137
Nook 21
Novel London 144–5

O

O'Bryan, Laurence 40
Old Tampa Book Company, US 139–40
online retailers 7–8, 35–7
see also Amazon
Osborne, Sandy 104–5

P

Parry, Edward 106
payment terms 129
Payne, Yvonne 50
Paypal 116
pitching books *see* approaches to booksellers
PJ Boox, Florida, US 52
POD (print-on-demand) 3–4, 41, 52, 71–2, 78, 92, 93, **249**
poetry slams 110
post-launch events 107–9
see also author events
pricing 31–2, 33, 84–5, 86–7
print rights, sale of 112–15
printing *see* color printing; litho printing; POD (print-on-demand)
production standards 79, 84–5, 91
public libraries 104, 121
public readings 109–10
see also author events
PublishDrive 21
publisher's imprints 81–2, **217**
publisher's reps 68, 70
publishing rights *see* print rights, sale of
Pulitzer, Joseph 113

Q

Quine, Rohan 77, 145

R

Rajakumar, Mohanalakshmi 138–40
Rakuten Kobo *see* Kobo
Rankin, Ian 89
readings, public 109–10
see also author events
restocks 89–90
returns *see* sale or return
Riggio, Len 46–7
Ross, Orna 16, 92, 112
royalties 34, 85, 93, 113, 123, **258**

S
sale or return 40, 66–7, 69, 125–8, 128–9
sales reps 68, 70
sample copies 63, 87
Sayburn Lane, Anna 54, 140–2
Schoen, Amy 55–6
Schwarz, Liesel 108
Shakespeare's Globe, theatre shop 54, 141–2
shelf displays, rearranging 89
Shepherd, Thomas 100
shipping software 117
show-rooming 36
signing books 144
Skea, Margaret 92–3, 142–3
SmashWords 21
Snell, Peter 40, 41, 78, 129
social media 63, 89, 97, 99, 104, 135, 136, 137, 148, **265**
Solomon, Nicola 130
Southwold Books, UK 9, 48
special editions 34
special orders 72–3, 121–2
special sales 10, 54–6, **266**
specialist bookstores 50–1
spine 78, **266**
Stanfords 50

Steen, Jane 120-1
Stormont, Anne 27, 128
Streetlib 21
subscription reading services 2, 3
Suffolk Anthology, Cheltenham, UK 39
Swift, Graham 133

T
Team Author UK 137
Tell Tales Books, Warrington, UK 137
Tolino 21
translations 112
transportation management systems (TMS) 117
travel-related books 50
Twitter 63, 135, 137, 148

U
United States, book industry 37-8
unusual bookstores 54

V
Vaughan Davies, Richard 143-4

W
Waterstones 8-9, 38-9, 47-8, 80
specific branches 45-6, 105-6, 136, 138, 145
websites, author 89, 104, 116-17, 136, 149, 151
Weldon, Tom 9
West End Lane Books, London, UK 134-5
Weybridge Bookshop, UK 9, 48
WH Smith 26-7, 106, 137, 143-4
wholesale distribution 69
wholesalers 70, 83, 84, 85-6, 117, 122, 123-4, 129, **282**
see also Gardners
WooCommerce 116
World Book Day 151

Write Blend, Liverpool, UK 136–7
Writers Plot Readers Read, Upper Hutt, NZ 135

Y
Young, Debbie 144–5
You've Got Mail (film) 46

THE END

ACKNOWLEDGMENTS

All good books are a team effort. An author's name goes on the cover but behind that is the creative team of editors and designers and formatters who made the book, the distributors and marketers who take it to readers, and the long list of supporters—from family members to work colleagues—without whom it would never have been created.

Then there are the other writers, from journalists and academics to storytellers and poets, who have published relevant ideas, information and inspirations that, quite literally, underwrite the book.

All this is true for this book you hold in your hand and our thanks to all those who had a hand in its making.

And finally to all at the Alliance of Independent Authors (ALLi). ALLi guides rely heavily on the work and wisdom of our members, ambassadors and advisors. The advice in our guides has often been published first on our blog, which they write, and draws also on their discussions in ALLi member forums, and on interviews with them about their writing and publishing experiences.

All of this is generously and freely shared with our non-profit CIC (Community Interest Company) with the intention of paying it forward, and benefitting other indie authors.

For this guide to Your Books in Bookstores , particular thanks to the creative team: Lauren Johnson, editor; Jane Dixon-Smith, cover design; and Sarah Begley for publishing assistance. And to our contributors:

Alison Morton
Andy Bromley
Anna Sayburn Lane
Anne Stormont

Barry Hutchison
Brooke Allen
Chris Longmuir
Dan Holloway
David Nicholls
Di Castle
Dianne Gardner
Edward Parry
Helena Halme
Jane Steen
John Doppler
Jonathan Hope
Jude Lennon
Karen Inglis
Katherine Hayton
Larry Garner
Lucienne Boyce
Margaret Skea
Mohanalakshmi Rajakumar
Nic Bottomley
Piers Alexander
Prue Batten
Richard Vaughan Davies
Ritesh Kala
Robin Cutler
Rosalind Minett
Sandy Osborne
Wendy Jones
Yvonne Payne

To them, and to all at ALLi: thank you for your generosity and for lighting the way.

JOIN ALLI

Alliance of Independent Authors

ALLi, the Alliance of Independent Authors is the global association for self-publishing indie authors.

Join us for reliable advice and advocacy, discounts, free guidebooks and resources, member forums, contract review, motivation, education and support from a wonderful indie author community.

AllianceIndependentAuthors.org

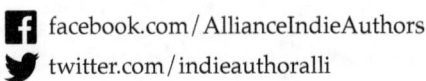

facebook.com/AllianceIndieAuthors
twitter.com/indieauthoralli

MORE ADVICE & FEEDBACK

ADVICE UPDATES FROM ALLI

Would you like to receive a weekly roundup of self-publishing advice from our award-winning blog?

Write more books. Reach more readers. Sell more Books.
Sign up for ALLi updates
Direct to your inbox each Wednesday

CREATIVE BUSINESS PLANNING MEMBERSHIP & WORKSHOPS

ALLi DIRECTOR ORNA ROSS RUNS A MONTHLY PAID MEMBERSHIP PROGRAM OFFERING SMALL-GROUP WORKSHOPS, DOWNLOADABLE PLANNERS, FACEBOOK ACCOUNTABILITY GROUP AND OTHER RESOURCES.

THIS IS A PAID PROGRAM THROUGH PATREON AND PLACES ARE LIMITED. FIND OUT MORE.

WE'D LOVE YOUR FEEDBACK
REVIEW REQUEST

If you enjoyed this book, would you consider leaving a brief review online on your favorite online bookstore that takes reviews: Amazon, Apple, Barnes and Noble Goodreads or Kobo?

A good review is very important to authors these days as it helps other readers know this is a book worth their time.

It doesn't have to be long or detailed. Just a sentence saying what you enjoyed and a star-rating is all that's needed. Many thanks.

Your Book in Bookstores: ALLi's Guide to Print Book Distribution for Authors

© DEBBIE P. YOUNG
ALLIANCE OF INDEPENDENT AUTHORS
2021

ebook: 978-1-913588-64-9
Paperback: 978-1-913588-65-6
Large Print: 978-1-913588-66-3
HB: 978-1-913588-67-0
Audio: 978-1-913588-68-7

THE MORAL RIGHTS OF THE AUTHOR HAVE BEEN ASSERTED.
ALL RIGHTS RESERVED.

ENQUIRIES: INFO@ORNAROSS.COM

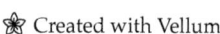 Created with Vellum

www.ingramcontent.com/pod-product-compliance
Lightning Source LLC
Chambersburg PA
CBHW070045230426
43661CB00005B/770